The
COMPLEX
PTSD
WORKBOOK

The
COMPLEX
PTSD
WORKBOOK

A Mind-Body Approach to Regaining Emotional Control & Becoming Whole

ARIELLE SCHWARTZ, PhD

Foreword by Jim Knipe, PhD

sheldon PRESS

First published by Althea Press, Berkeley, California in 2016

First published in Great Britain by Sheldon Press in 2020
An imprint of John Murray Press
A division of Hodder & Stoughton Ltd,
An Hachette UK company

8

This book is for information or educational purposes only and is not intended
to act as a substitute for medical advice or treatment. Any person with a
condition requiring medical attention should consult a qualified
medical practitioner or suitable therapist.

A CIP catalogue record for this title is available from the British Library

Trade Paperback ISBN 9781529312133
eBook ISBN 9781529312157

Printed and bound in Great Britain by Clays Ltd, Elcograf S.p.A.

John Murray Press policy is to use papers that are natural, renewable
and recyclable products and made from wood grown in sustainable
forests. The logging and manufacturing processes are expected to
conform to the environmental regulations of the country of origin.

John Murray Press
Carmelite House
50 Victoria Embankment
London EC4Y 0DZ

www.sheldonpress.co.uk

To my children, Eliana and Ian.

Thank you for the gift of being your mother.
You are my teachers about the most important
lesson in life: what it means to love.

Contents

Foreword

A breakthrough moment in psychotherapy can be an insight or a shift toward adaptive resolution of a disturbing memory; or it can occur in an early therapy session, or even prior to the first session, when the client makes the brave decision to pick up the phone and make an initial appointment. This book is written for individuals who are at the initial point of turning the corner on their long-standing problems and have questions: "I know generally what psychotherapy is, but what would it be for me, and how could it really help me?" "There are so many different kinds of therapy—which method would be the best fit for me?" "What would an actual therapy session be like for me, with the difficulties I have?" This book contains concise, accurate, and accessible answers to these types of questions.

The theme throughout the chapters is one of *normalizing* the problems of people with difficult and extensive trauma histories—those individuals who might be described within the categories of complex PTSD and/or developmental trauma disorder. Dr. Schwartz makes it clear that complex PTSD is a normal response or adaptation to non-normal life conditions that may be in a person's history. This in itself is a very useful perspective, especially for those clients who have been struggling with emotional problems for a long time, and, as a result, have much reduced self-esteem. The comprehensive and compassionate descriptions of the many different manifestations of complex PTSD are likely to be helpful for those clients who have feared, erroneously, that they are too unusual or "weird" to be helped.

Throughout each of the chapters, the reader is invited to respond in writing with information from their own life experience. This volume then becomes more than just a book off the shelf, but instead a more real and interactive experience.

The chapters provide comprehensive coverage of a range of issues related to the treatment of complex PTSD: the importance of attachment patterns (as a sometimes hidden element of an adult's emotional problem); an overview of different models of treatment, with enough information about each method so the reader can make an informed choice regarding which approach might be the best fit; and potential obstacles to successful treatment—obstacles that can be identified in advance so that an appropriate treatment plan can be constructed. With these issues in mind, the therapist and client will be better able to form a roadmap for therapy, a contract listing therapy goals, and the likely best path to reaching each of those goals. This book is a valuable resource for all those affected by complex PTSD, allowing them to be informed and active as partners in the therapeutic healing process.

JIM KNIPE, PhD

Introduction

I t takes tremendous courage to confront childhood trauma. Like searching in the dark for an unknown source of pain, the process of healing can feel daunting, if not terrifying. This book will help you illuminate that darkness and enter a new world of personal freedom.

Childhood traumas can range from having faced extreme violence and neglect to having confronted feelings of not belonging, being unwanted, or being chronically misunderstood. You may have grown up in an environment where your curiosity and enthusiasm were constantly devalued. Perhaps you were brought up in a family where your parents had unresolved traumas of their own, which impaired their ability to attend to your emotional needs. Or, you may have faced vicious sexual or physical attacks. In all such situations, you learn to compensate by developing defenses around your most vulnerable parts. Importantly, we cannot compare one person's loss or pain to another's—every person's experience is different and leaves different wounds.

Unresolved childhood trauma has significant consequences on mental and emotional health. You might alternate between feeling cut off and feeling flooded with emotions such as fear, anger, or despair. Perhaps you suffer from anxiety or depression. Maybe you resort to disconnection or dissociation to get through the day. Relationships are often compromised. Your physical health may also be impacted by illness or chronic pain. If you find yourself struggling with any of these symptoms, this book is for you.

Healing childhood trauma involves a balance: attending to the wounds of the past while living in the present. Simply attending to the demands of daily living can feel insurmountable at times. Going to the store to buy groceries, handling stress at work, raising children, or relating to your spouse can feel overwhelming when you are flooded with anxiety or shut down in shame. Having strategies to remain mindful and feel grounded is essential. These tools will allow you to turn toward your pain without creating additional distress.

As a therapist, I have spent years helping those with histories of childhood trauma find their way to wholeness. I know the territory of the healing path, having walked it myself. This book provides a map to the terrain, along with a knowledgeable and compassionate guide.

Within this book you will learn all about complex PTSD and gain valuable insight into the types of symptoms associated with unresolved childhood trauma. My goal is to empower you with a thorough understanding of the science and psychology of trauma so you can make informed choices about therapy and partner with your health care providers. You will be guided to develop positive strategies to replace destructive behaviors. Mindfulness-based experiential practices will help you develop both self-acceptance and a sense of safety—which will prepare you to explore your traumatic past. Overall, this book offers a strength-based perspective to integrate positive beliefs and behaviors.

> Within the ground of another—in this case, a compassionate therapist—you embrace experiences of confusion, discomfort, anger, grief, shame, and pain.

Focusing on self-care—including yoga, journaling, and other valuable practices—can enable you to create routines that facilitate lifelong wellness.

This book is not a substitute for therapy. Recovery from developmental trauma requires that you have a reparative experience *in a relationship*. Within the ground of another—in this case, a compassionate therapist—you embrace experiences of confusion, discomfort, anger, grief, shame, and pain. A compassionate therapist offers a container of sorts for the feelings and memories that you might be unable to handle alone. And together, you'll build trust, gain perspective, and find healing tools that work best for you. Still, the words in this book will guide you to tap into the healing power that exists inside of you. Using this book along-side psychotherapy can help educate and deepen understanding to reduce the time and cost of treatment.

I invite you to think about your healing journey as a deeply rewarding, lifelong process of self-discovery that you deserve. Undoubtedly, there will be pain and suffering. Yet, self-acknowledgment also offers keys to empowerment and personal freedom. Throughout these pages you will find a strength-based, nonstigmatizing approach to healing. You are not broken, in need of fixing. Rather, you are deeply hurt, in need of care. With sufficient support, you will be able to release your defensive self-protection to reveal your innate worth, wisdom, and creativity—your greatness. I invite you to discover and be surprised by your resilience. You have a history that has endowed you with a unique perspective on what it means to be alive. Only you can decide what to do with your life now, and you're on the right track. You're here.

CHAPTER ONE

Understanding Trauma

If you were neglected or abused as a child, your primary orientation to the world is likely to be one of threat, fear, and survival. It's only natural that a childhood experience with untrustworthy parents or caregivers would leave you untrusting or confused about what constitutes a loving relationship. Fear and lack of safety might compel you to continuously scan your environment for potential threats. You may have relied upon coping strategies to survive, such as dissociation, a protective mechanism that disconnects you from threatening experiences. If you can relate to these qualities, you may also identify with related issues such as self-criticism, emotional suffering, and relationship difficulties. If this describes you, it is not your fault and you have not failed. You have a form of post-traumatic stress disorder (PTSD).

Traumatic experiences are, by their very definition, frightening and over-whelming. PTSD is often associated with events such as car accidents, natural disasters, or acts of violence. It is common after experiences like these to feel flooded with powerful emotions such as fear or sadness, and to begin avoiding situations that remind you of the trauma. PTSD refers to the presence of these symptoms well after the event is over. However, there is another kind of post-traumatic stress called complex PTSD (C-PTSD), which occurs as a result of long-term exposure to traumatic stress, rather than in response to a single incident. C-PTSD typically arises as a result of ongoing stress or repeated traumatic events that occur during childhood and is sometimes referred to as developmental trauma disorder (DTD).

Growing up afraid has ramifications on cognitive, emotional, and physical development that can persist into adulthood—until you have the necessary support to heal your wounds. C-PTSD is not a character weakness; it is a learned stress disorder. The good news is this: You can reclaim your life from the costs of childhood trauma. When you are empowered with knowledge and awareness, you can deepen your self-acceptance and reduce the difficult emotions that often accompany developmental trauma. In this chapter and throughout this book, you will develop a greater understanding of complex PTSD and discover ways to mitigate its effects to help you heal. The goals of this workbook are to encourage a compassionate understanding of your symptoms and to provide you with action steps that will help you recover from developmental trauma.

> Take comfort in this: C-PTSD is the result of learned ineffective beliefs and behaviors that can be replaced by a positive mind-set and health-promoting behaviors.

Learning Self-Care

By the time I met Diane, her suffering had become unbearable. She reported experiencing debilitating anxiety mixed with feelings of hopelessness and despair. She was married, but her relationship was suffering under the weight of her symptoms. In the past year, she had gained weight, developed migraines, and struggled with insomnia.

Diane was very skilled at avoiding dealing with her traumatic past. To survive, she had learned to bury her painful feelings and memories, preferring not to talk about her childhood. It simply hurt too much. She kept a tight lid on her past, but now her migraines and insomnia made her feel as though she were coming apart at the seams. Diane had lost a sense of choice or control over her emotional life.

I learned that Diane had a history of exposure to domestic violence during her childhood. Her father was an alcoholic and her mother was never really involved in her life, other than to tell her what she was doing wrong. With tears streaming down her cheeks, she said, "They never should have had children; I should have never been born."

If you can relate to Diane's story in any way, take comfort in this: C-PTSD is the result of *learned* ineffective beliefs and behaviors that can be replaced by a positive mind-set and health-promoting behaviors. With the same tools that you'll find in this book, Diane was able to integrate resources such as mindfulness and relaxation techniques into her life to help her feel more grounded and safe. She explored her history and developed a greater tolerance for facing her painful emotions. Writing about her past allowed her to feel in control of her life now. As a result of her consistent commitment to self-care, she strengthened her self-acceptance and compassion.

After several weeks of practicing the action steps that you'll learn in this book, Diane had an epiphany: *"My parents neglected me, and now I neglect myself by not taking care of my body as an adult. They could not love me the way that I needed, but I can become good at loving myself!"*

IN PRACTICE

In what ways can you relate to Diane's story? Take some time to write down any associations you have.

_____

_____

_____

_____

_____

_____

_____

_____

_____

_____

_____

_____

_____

_____

_____

_____

_____

_____

_____

_____

_____

_____

_____

_____

_____

EMBRACING CHANGE

It is human nature to seek safety and stability. You might say, "This is who I am, and this is who I will always be." Familiar, repeated routines simplify life and conserve energy. They can help manage stress, because there is comfort in what is known. New situations require more awareness of our surroundings. Some routines may temporarily reduce stress, but can lead to unwanted consequences and unhealthy habits such as obesity, procrastination, self-sabotage, or addictions.

In order to embrace any change, we need to take specific action to challenge behaviors and beliefs that no longer serve us. Research suggests that creating any desired change in life requires the repeated practice of new health-promoting behaviors until they become new habits. Getting regular exercise, eating a healthy diet, and developing positive social connections are among the best things we can do for ourselves to strengthen our resilience. No matter what you have gone through, you have the ability to heal your body and mind.

The tricky part is this: Once you allow yourself to feel your pain—to face it head-on—you can free yourself from it. When you recognize that limiting beliefs are running your life, you can then work to take charge of your mind and begin reclaiming your right to a positive outlook on life.

A Heavy Burden

Fred has been living with anxiety for much of his life. Now an adult, he has two children who depend on him and a job that he can't afford to lose. After his chest pains started last year, he told his doctor about his ongoing panic attacks and insomnia. He was prescribed anti-anxiety medications, which kept him afloat but left him feeling flat and depressed. Thankfully, his doctor also suggested that he seek psychotherapy. As we explored his past, he spoke of growing up in a chaotic and unpredictable childhood home. He said that after his parent's divorce, his mother was never the same. Slowly, we unpacked the heavy burden of insecurity that Fred has been carrying all this time.

Complex PTSD is a set of symptoms that are the result of pain and stress that often begin at a very early age—they could be all you've known. Naturally, these early experiences shape your perspective of yourself and the world. Healing asks that you turn toward your past to find relief from the weight of trauma. As a result, you become less defined by your history and have greater choice about your future.

C-PTSD can be the result of the following types of experiences:

- Childhood relationships with parents or caregivers that are frightening, unpredictable, and/or overwhelming
- Ongoing or repeated experiences of neglect or physical, verbal, or sexual abuse
- Growing up with exposure to domestic violence
- Being raised by a caregiver who has an active addiction or untreated mental illness
- Experiencing abuse at especially vulnerable times of development, such as early childhood or adolescence
- Facing severe social stress such as bullying, disability, or exposure to traumatic events within your community without support by a caregiver who protects and cares for you
- Being discriminated against or feeling disempowered without a caregiver who helps advocate for you or takes responsibility for your needs

However painful it might seem at first, unpacking the burdens of your traumatic history can be thought of as profound self-care. As if moving into a larger, more spacious home, you are unpacking the painful memories of the past, and making room for more positive emotions. In the process of unpacking, you want to pace yourself so you do not get overwhelmed. You bring stories of pain out of hiding into the light of your awareness. By allowing each memory to find its right place, each one can be reviewed, understood, and worked through.

COMMON MISDIAGNOSES

Many people with a history of complex PTSD and dissociation have been misunderstood, misdiagnosed, and inappropriately medicated. Here are some reasons why:

1. **C-PTSD is not included in the *DSM-5*:** Despite much deliberation, neither C-PTSD nor DTD was added to the latest version of the *DSM-5* (*Diagnostic and Statistical Manual of Mental Disorders, Fifth Edition*) used by clinicians. The diagnosis listed for PTSD most closely matches the symptoms and effects of C-PTSD, because more than 90 percent of the symptoms are the same.

2. **Co-occurring diagnoses can mask C-PTSD:** Accurate diagnosis sometimes is difficult because disorders can exist simultaneously, known as co-occurrence. For example, children who were neglected or abused are at higher risk for anxiety disorders, depressive disorders, and learning disabilities. Children with these disorders are also at greater risk for abuse.

3. **C-PTSD symptoms look like other disorders:** The symptoms of C-PTSD can mimic symptoms of other disorders. For example, a child or teen who has been abused or neglected might appear impulsive, anxious, angry, and/or depressed. But if a thorough family history is not understood, it can lead to inaccurate diagnoses of bipolar disorder, anxiety disorder, or major depressive disorder.

Here are some common mistaken or co-occurring diagnoses:

- Borderline personality disorder or other personality disorders
- Bipolar disorder
- Attention deficit hyperactivity disorder (ADHD)
- Sensory processing disorder
- Learning disabilities
- Anxiety disorders
- Major depressive disorder or dysphoria
- Somatization disorders (experiencing psychological disorders as physical symptoms)
- Substance abuse or dependence

An essential component of healing involves working with a psychotherapist, psychiatrist, or medical doctor to determine an accurate diagnosis. A proper diagnosis is not meant to cause shame; rather, it is meant to point you in the right direction for recovery and healing.

Eight Contributing Factors to the Development of C-PTSD

Why will two people with similar histories have different outcomes? Why is it that multiple children can grow up in the same household, but only one feel traumatized? The development and expression of C-PTSD is multifaceted, and is not just influenced by exposure to childhood trauma. Let's look at why some people may be more susceptible to developing an adverse reaction to trauma than others:

1 **Intensity, duration, and timing:** Needless to say, the longer the abuse or trauma continues and the greater its intensity, the greater the likelihood you will develop C-PTSD. It is also important to consider the timing of the traumatic stress. Children are most susceptible to the impact of such stressors during critical growth periods, such as the first three years of life when the nervous system is extremely fragile and during adolescence when they are forming their identity.

2 **Genetics:** Research indicates that anxiety disorders, including PTSD, tend to run in families. While not a direct cause of PTSD, having a parent with PTSD is associated with a greater risk for the development of PTSD after exposure to a trauma. Research suggests that there is a biological predisposition among these children.

3 **Environment:** Parents with PTSD respond differently to their children, resulting in greater disruptions in care and attachment. Mothers with PTSD tend to be both overprotective and overreactive, which can result in children feeling both intruded upon and abandoned. As children respond in fear or anger, an environmental cycle of abuse can occur, in which a parent may become increasingly abusive.

4 **In-utero influence:** Infants born to mothers who were pregnant during a traumatic event that could have resulted in a diagnosis of PTSD (such as during the 9/11 attacks) had lower birth weights and decreased levels of cortisols (chemicals that respond to stress). Although this does not necessarily result in childhood abuse or neglect, such infants can be harder to soothe, more prone to colic, and at increased risk for PTSD.

5 **Family dynamics:** Parents develop different relationships with different children. Factors that influence this bond with a child can include such things as comfort level with a child's gender, readiness to have a child, and events surrounding the pregnancy or birth. For example, unplanned or unwanted pregnancies can lead to resentment or anger toward a child, or a difficult pregnancy or traumatic birthing process might cause a parent to reject or blame a child.

6 **Modeling:** Children who grow up in abusive homes tend to be exposed to multiple risk factors. Medical care may not be consistent. There may be insufficient modeling of hygiene practices, or a lack of encouragement of health-promoting behaviors such as exercise or healthy eating. There may also be excessive modeling of high-risk behaviors like smoking or substance abuse.

7 **Presence of a learning disability or ADHD:** There is a strong correlation between children with learning disabilities, including Attention Deficit/ Hyperactivity Disorder (ADHD) and child abuse. This connection appears to be bidirectional. Children who are abused are at greater risk for the development of learning disabilities because of the impact of chronic stress and trauma on their developing brain. Additionally, children who have a learning disability or ADHD are at greater risk of being abused when parents misunderstand or are triggered by their child's cognitive differences, distractibility, or impulsivity.

8 **Lack of resilience factors:** Resilience factors are those protective resources, such as parents, that alleviate the impact of childhood trauma. Research suggests that when parents are not supportive, even an attachment to an adult in your community who understands, nurtures, and protects you can lessen the impact of traumatic childhood events. Additional protective factors include participation in activities outside of the home and developing positive peer relationships. When resilience factors are lacking, the impact of neglect or abuse can be amplified by a feeling that those around you have failed to protect you.

ATTACHMENT THEORY AND C-PTSD

Attachment theory describes how young children respond when they're separated from their primary caregiver. *Attachment* is defined as an emotional bond between two people, initially a caregiver and an infant, which provides a foundation for healthy relationships later in life. Secure attachment forms when we can depend on a safe, predictable, attuned, and loving caregiver during infancy and early childhood. When caregivers are attuned, they are able to read the cues that signal a child's needs.

Sometimes an infant's cry is hard to understand. Is the baby hungry, tired, or simply needing to be held? Importantly, parenting does not need to be "perfect"—it never is! "Good enough" caregivers will inevitably misattune to their children on occasion, and these mistakes provide healthy opportunities to learn that ruptures in connection can be repaired. This type of parenting produces what is generally referred to as *secure attachment*. Secure attachment provides the home base that allows a child to feel confident to explore their world. Healthy attachment is associated with the ability to learn emotion regulation and stress tolerance, and the development of healthy boundaries. For example, if a mother and her one-year-old child go to the park, the child will initially remain close to mother for a short period of time, and then run off to explore.

The neglect and early childhood abuse that can accompany complex PTSD are not associated with secure attachment. Years of research by Dr. John Bowlby and Dr. Mary Ainsworth identify patterns of insecure and anxious attachment styles:

- **Insecure ambivalent:** The insecure ambivalent child has grown up with an inconsistent primary caregiver, who is at times highly responsive and perceptive, but can also be intrusive and invasive. The child cannot depend upon the caregiver for predictable attunement and connection, and consequently develops uncertainty and anxiety. Insecure ambivalent adults tend to feel overly dependent and suffer from abandonment anxiety and an overall sense that relationships are unreliable.

- **Insecure avoidant:** The insecure avoidant child has grown up with a distant or disengaged caregiver who is repeatedly emotionally unavailable and rejecting. As a result, this child adapts by avoiding closeness, disconnecting emotionally, or becoming overly self-reliant. Insecure avoidant adults tend to have grown up to be dismissive of their own and other people's emotions and face challenges when their partners long for a deeper, more intimate connection.

- **Disorganized:** The most disturbing attachment settings result in a disorganized attachment style. This child has grown up with a primary caregiver whose behavior is overwhelming, chaotic, and/or abusive. The caregiver is a source of alarm and confusion, resulting in a paradox related to the child's biological drive to seek closeness from the very source of the terror that they are trying to escape. This is often referred to as "fright without solution," an unsolvable dilemma for the child. Disorganized adults tend to rely upon impulsive or aggressive behaviors to manage uncomfortable emotions. Relationship interactions can mimic the abuse they experienced during childhood with caregivers. They might act abusive themselves or choose abusive partners because it feels familiar.

C-PTSD is associated with all of these attachment styles.

IN PRACTICE

Which of the previous contributing factors of C-PTSD might you say relate to your life?

_____

_____

_____

_____

_____

_____

_____

_____

_____

_____

How C-PTSD Affects the Mind and Body

Children require consistency. Caregivers who are predictable help children develop clear expectations about themselves and the world. Such predictability provides a groundwork of safety and allows a child to adapt to the many inner changes they go through during early development. But this isn't the case in a household of neglect or abuse.

C-PTSD often arises out of interactions that occur in the first years of life. Sometimes the trauma begins within the first months of being born. Such early childhood memories are not like typical memories that occur later in life. You may not have images or a clear story. Instead, you might experience emotions without understanding why, or even physical sensations of unknown origin.

Growing up afraid has ramifications on all aspects of development—cognitive, emotional, and physical. The costs of childhood trauma can persist into adulthood until you find sufficient support to heal your past. The most common experiences among individuals with C-PTSD include:

- **Cognitive distortions:** These include inaccurate beliefs about oneself, others, and the world.
- **Emotional distress:** Frequent feelings of being overwhelmed, anxiety, helplessness, hopelessness, despair, deep loneliness, shame, unfairness, injustice, and depression and suicidal thoughts are often triggered by social loss, abandonment, and disconnection.
- **Disturbing somatic sensations:** Historical threats are maintained as uncomfortable body sensations or somatization, in which psychological distress presents in the form of physical symptoms.
- **Disorientation:** Inaccurate beliefs, emotions, and body sensations contribute to a loss of distinction between the past and the present.
- **Hypervigilance:** High sensitivity to tracking nuances and subtleties in body language and facial expressions within other people is developed as an attempt to keep oneself safe.
- **Avoidance:** Avoidance involves learned patterns of shutting out or pushing away uncomfortable sensations, memories, or emotions. This is often maintained by defenses such as denial, repression, dissociation, or addictive behaviors.

OTHER SYMPTOMS OF C-PTSD

Additional symptoms that are common among individuals with C-PTSD include:

- Feelings of irritability
- Self-harm/self-injury, such as cutting one's own skin or pulling hair out
- Eating disorders, such as binge eating, bulimia, and anorexia
- Emotional eating
- Social anxiety, agoraphobia, or paranoia
- Difficulty concentrating
- Impulsivity or recklessness
- Excessive risk-taking and promiscuity
- Outbursts of anger
- Suicidal thoughts, plans, or attempts
- Addiction
- Difficulty maintaining a job

A diagnosis is a good thing, not a bad thing. Keep in mind that an accurate diagnosis becomes a part of your growing toolbox of knowledge that will help you better understand yourself and move forward with wisdom. A diagnosis can allow you and your treatment providers to work together to face and address your symptoms.

- **Interpersonal problems:** Ineffective interpersonal relationship dynamics include withdrawing from, blaming, pushing away, or criticizing friends and loved ones unnecessarily. Patterns learned within dysfunctional family systems tend to get repeated in adulthood until new and effective interpersonal strategies are developed.
- **Brain development:** Abuse and neglect produce measurable changes in brain structures that are associated with deficits in social skills and academic success.
- **Health problems:** Unresolved C-PTSD is a significant cause of physical health concerns in adulthood.

Mental and Emotional Symptoms

The primary emotional and cognitive symptoms of C-PTSD are a combination of avoidance symptoms, intrusive symptoms, and depressive symptoms. It is best to think of emotions as a combination of three forces: environment, body awareness or "felt sense," and the mind, which makes meaning out of experiences based upon memories from the past. When you rely too heavily upon your trauma-related feelings, it is common to react as if you are being hurt in the present moment, when in fact you actually are loved and safe. As a result, you might jump too quickly to conclusions without pause for reflection. These inaccurate interpretations of events tend to lead to painful losses that could have otherwise been avoided.

Jan struggled with strong feelings that influenced her interpretation of current events. For example, after work her husband liked to watch TV as a way to decompress from a long day. Jan began to feel unimportant. "You don't really love me," she insisted angrily. When her husband turned off the TV and tried to connect, she pushed him away, saying, "If you really cared about me I wouldn't have to beg for your attention!" Shrugging his shoulders, her husband felt unable to help Jan feel his love for her.

In some situations, you might feel emotionally overwhelmed. When you are "flooded," you will have a hard time effectively thinking your way through any situation. In fact, the emotion centers of the brain will activate, reducing brain activity in the parts responsible for rational thought processes and making decisions. Behaviors then become impulsive, rather than reflective choices.

Overreactive responses sit at one end of the emotions continuum. When you have a childhood history of abuse or neglect, it is also common to deny, dissociate, or shut down from pain. Lack of attention to your emotional world will leave you feeling disoriented. If you are intolerant of emotions, you will likely feel cut off, like something is missing, or as if you are just going through the motions.

Emotions help give us purpose, meaning, and the experience of being alive. The butterflies in your stomach, lump in your throat, beating of your heart, and the warmth in your face give you feedback about yourself and your world.

The aim is to find a balance between thinking and feeling in order to have healthy empathy, develop successful relationships, and make effective decisions.

Let's look at the emotional and cognitive symptoms of C-PTSD:

AVOIDANCE SYMPTOMS

Kevin has smoked pot for many years. Now his wife wants to have a child and has asked him to stop. Reluctantly he came to therapy after his wife threatened that if he didn't stop, she would leave him. Exploring Kevin's childhood history, I learned of his father's anger and rage. Kevin shrugged his shoulders, stating casually, "Yeah, he pushed me around, but it's not a big deal." Within the safety of therapy, we began to acknowledge that indeed his father's behaviors had a significant impact on his emotional life. He began to address his own anger about his childhood.

In order to get away from memories of childhood trauma, it is common to develop avoidance strategies. Sometimes this involves avoiding situations, people, and places that serve as reminders of the past. Avoidance is also maintained by defenses such as denying the past, repressing feelings, idealizing parents, minimizing the pain, or dissociating. It is common to use substances or maintain other addictive behaviors such as emotional eating or excessive exercising to avoid feeling pain.

INTRUSIVE SYMPTOMS

"Get away from me!" screamed Helen in the middle of the night. Another nightmare woke her up from a deep sleep. She has been haunted by these dreams for as long as she can remember. Helen came into my office because she had not been able to concentrate on her college classes. For the first time, she began to talk about her father and how uncomfortable she was when he would come into her room at night. She needed somebody to help her sort out what happened.

UNDERSTANDING DISSOCIATION

Dissociation, like all other symptoms of C-PTSD, is a learned behavior that initially helped you cope with a threatening environment. A neglected or abused child will rely upon built-in, biological protection mechanisms for survival to "tune out" threatening experiences. In adulthood, dissociation becomes a well-maintained division between the part of you involved in keeping up with daily tasks of living and the part of you that is holding emotions of fear, shame, or anger. You might feel that it's just too much to think about what happened.

When emotions or body sensations come to the surface of your awareness, it is common to instinctively push the scary, yucky, painful, or confusing feelings far away by resorting to learned dissociative patterns. Symptoms of dissociation exist on a continuum, and can be relatively mild such as feeling foggy or fuzzy, having a hard time talking about experiences, or feeling tired. You might feel distracted or have difficulty concentrating. You might feel numb or cut off. More intense symptoms include feeling out of control, having lapses of memory, or experiencing "lost time."

You can heal dissociation by developing the capacity to recognize that traumatic events happened to you and that they are over now. You develop .the capacity to realize that traumatic events influence your sense of self and your basic assumptions about the world. Healing dissociation involves differentiating between the past and the present, and you can do so by cultivating mindful awareness of the "here and now" (see page 141).

"Re-experiencing" symptoms, such as anxiety, flashbacks, hypervigilance, or nightmares, is among the most common disturbances in individuals with PTSD. Hypervigilance involves being on guard or highly sensitized to your surroundings in order to keep yourself safe. Re-experiencing symptoms related to early childhood memories—from before you could even speak—may come in the form of a vague uncomfortable "felt sense" or physical pain. High arousal symptoms, characterized by feelings such as anxiety, aggression, and irritability, are often experienced by individuals with C-PTSD. These often manifest in what is known as emotional dysregulation, or sweeping emotions of sadness, rage, or fear. These can feel intrusive or even hijack your relationship to yourself, your family, and your world, and can result in feeling stuck in patterns of disconnection, resentment, or abandonment with family and friends.

DEPRESSIVE SYMPTOMS

Andrew grew up in a home where he felt responsible for his alcoholic mother. Sadly, she never recovered despite his many attempts to help her. As an adult, he continues to feel ineffective at work. When he receives any critical feedback from his boss, he feels deeply rejected and thinks, "What is the point of trying?"

High arousal symptoms are one side of the C-PTSD equation. Low arousal symptoms, such as hopelessness, despair, and depression, reside on the other side. These symptoms typically result from living in a threatening environment with no escape. When you have no ability to change your situation, you may be left feeling ineffective, powerless, and helpless. Shame and unworthiness are signature depressive symptoms of C-PTSD.

IN PRACTICE

The following questions will help identify your own emotional and cognitive symptoms of C-PTSD:

What avoidance symptoms (denial, repression, idealization, minimization, addictions, dissociation) do you experience? In what way(s) do these symptoms get in the way of you living the life you want?

_____

_____

_____

_____

_____

_____

What intrusive symptoms (anxiety, flashbacks, nightmares, hypervigilance, emotional dysregulation, interpersonal problems) do you experience? In what way(s) do these symptoms interfere with your life now?

_____

_____

_____

_____

_____

_____

_____

_____

_____

_____

_____

_____

_____

_____

_____

_____

_____

_____

_____

_____

_____

_____

_____

_____

_____

RECOGNIZING SHAME

Shame is characterized by the belief that you are "bad." This emotion is based upon a distorted sense of yourself as being unworthy, damaged, or a failure. Young children are completely dependent upon caregivers for a sense of safety and connection in the world. When parents are frightening, abusive, or unavailable, children can feel confused about who is at fault. When children witness something bad, they feel bad. Inaccurate and judgmental thoughts such as the following ones perpetuate shame:

- "There must be something wrong with me!"
- "I'm so stupid."
- "I can't seem to do anything right."
- "I'm an emotional wreck."
- "I'm just lazy."

Once you are aware of the messages you are telling yourself, you can do something about them and you will develop the strength to turn toward your pain. The self-compassion and acceptance practices you will discover in this workbook are antidotes to shame.

What depressive symptoms (hopelessness, despair, depression, powerlessness, lack of self-efficacy, helplessness, shame, unworthiness) do you experience? How do these symptoms show themselves in your life?

_____

_____

_____

_____

_____

_____

_____

_____

Physical Symptoms

Unresolved trauma can take a significant toll on your physical health. Unresolved *childhood* trauma is particularly insidious, with effects that are both gradual and cumulative. Having an understanding of how your body responds to stress and trauma can empower you to partner with your treatment providers and actively attend to your physical health care needs. Let's take a closer look at the relationship between stress and your health.

When we're under any stress, the nervous system will initiate a fight-or-flight response as an attempt to reestablish safety and connection. The Center on the Developing Child at Harvard University recognizes three forms of childhood stress:

1 **Positive stress response:** A healthy stress response is one that is temporary and resolves itself with a positive connection to loving caregivers. Examples of healthy stressors during childhood include adapting to a new child-care provider, or brief and tolerable separations from the primary caregiver. Healthy stress actually tones the nervous system to cope with stressful situations encountered in adulthood.

2 **Tolerable stress response:** Here you might face a significant single-incident trauma as a child, such as a fire or the death of a loved one. However, if you have a supportive environment with loving caregivers who help you process your experience, such an event is actually associated with the development of positive coping skills in adulthood.

3 **Toxic stress response:** In this case, profound or ongoing traumatic events take place without support from loving adults. These situations are associated with a negative outcome on emotional and physical health in adulthood.

Ideally, stress is temporary. However, when a stressful situation persists, it can result in the body remaining in a state of high alert without the ability to rest. Traumatic stress is the result of an event that has life-threatening implications, in which you become immobilized without a way to escape. In such a situation, the fight-or-flight response was unsuccessful and you were left feeling helpless.

During any stressful event, the body will produce cortisols, the chemicals associated with the sympathetic nervous system and the fight-or-flight response.

When stress is ongoing, the body will continue to produce high amounts of stress chemicals. In contrast, unresolved C-PTSD is actually associated with chronically low levels of cortisols within the bloodstream. This does not mean that your body is producing fewer cortisols. In fact, the body continues to release high amounts of stress chemicals; however, the physiology of unresolved PTSD involves a change in how your body processes these cortisols. As a result, PTSD is associated with frequent bursts of cortisol and chronically low levels of available cortisols in the bloodstream. This is the physiological explanation of the classic alternation between feeling overwhelmed and shut down. It is as if you are driving with one foot on the gas and one on the brakes.

The *autonomic nervous system* (ANS) plays a significant role in our emotional and physiological responses to stress and trauma. The ANS is understood to have two primary systems: the sympathetic nervous system and the parasympathetic nervous system. The *sympathetic nervous system* is associated with the fight-or-flight response, and the release of cortisols throughout the bloodstream. The *parasympathetic nervous system* puts the brakes on the sympathetic nervous system, so the body stops releasing stress chemicals and shifts toward relaxation, digestion, and regeneration. The sympathetic and parasympathetic nervous systems are meant to work in a rhythmic alternation that supports healthy digestion, sleep, and immune system functioning. However, chronic stress and unresolved C-PTSD can interfere with the balance between the sympathetic and parasympathetic nervous systems, which impacts physical health.

CHRONIC STRESS, TRAUMA, AND HEALTH

There exists an inverse relationship between stress chemicals (bloodstream cortisol levels) and immune system functioning. When bloodstream cortisol levels are high, the immune system is suppressed. In contrast, when bloodstream cortisol levels are low, the immune system is enhanced or "unchecked." The immune system is associated with inflammation in the body. This inflammation is necessary when we are fighting off a virus or bacteria. However, when the immune system continues to inflame without a target, there is a greater likelihood of long-term physical health problems.

Health problems associated with chronic stress, in which cortisols are high and immunity is suppressed, include:

- **High blood pressure:** Blood pressure is increased, which is associated with hypertension and heart disease.
- **Blood sugar imbalances:** Blood sugar remains elevated to maintain a fight-or-flight response, leading to increased risk for hypoglycemia and diabetes.
- **Food cravings:** Cravings for sweets, carbs, salt, vinegar, and spices can lead to emotional eating when they continue over time.
- **Addictions:** It is common to seek out temporary stress relief from the quick fix of alcohol, caffeine, nicotine, or other drugs, contributing to the development of unhealthy habits.
- **Sluggish digestion:** Chronic stress interferes with digestion, because digestion is a nonessential activity when we need to flee or fight a predator, and so it shuts down when the body is stressed.
- **Suppressed immunity:** Ongoing suppressed immunity is associated with an increased susceptibility to disease and cancer.

Health problems associated with unresolved PTSD, in which bloodstream cortisols are low and immunity is unchecked, include:

- **Digestive disturbances:** The parasympathetic nervous system is associated with enhanced digestion. However, too much of a good thing can wreak havoc. In the case of chronic PTSD, there is an overproduction of stomach acids and a greater likelihood of digestive conditions such as acid reflux and irritable bowel syndrome.
- **Sleep disturbances:** Normally, cortisol rises rapidly after we wake, gradually falls over the day, rises again in the late afternoon, and then falls again, reaching a low point in the middle of the night. The circadian rhythm, or our body's clock, is patterned through the cortisol rhythm. With chronic PTSD, there is an abnormally flattened circadian cortisol cycle that has been linked to fatigue and insomnia.
- **Autoimmune disorders:** When there is no virus or bacteria that needs to be fought, the unchecked immune system will target healthy tissue, leading to increased vulnerability to autoimmune disorders.

THE ACE STUDY

The psychological and medical fields are now recognizing that children exposed to trauma are significantly more likely to have physical health risk factors later in life. The Adverse Childhood Experiences (ACE) study, conducted through Kaiser Permanente, assessed 17,000 patients' experiences of childhood trauma, including:

- Physical abuse
- Verbal abuse
- Sexual abuse
- Physical or emotional neglect
- Exposure to domestic violence
- Exposure to household members who were substance abusers
- Exposure to household members who were mentally ill, suicidal, or imprisoned

The study applied a score to participants for each ACE factor they had experienced. The results of the study indicate that having one ACE factor was highly predictive of having other ACE factors. Experiencing any one of these categories places a child at risk, but having lived through four or more ACE factors appears to be a critical mass of stress. Felitti et al. (1998) collaborated with the CDC (Centers for Disease Control and Prevention) to understand the degree of risk. They concluded that adults who had been exposed to four ACE factors as children are 4 times more likely to become depressed, 7 times more likely to use substances, and 12 times more likely to attempt suicide than adults with an ACE score of zero. These individuals are more likely to experience social, emotional, and cognitive impairments, and are at greater risk for physical illnesses such as heart disease, cancer, chronic lung disease, and liver disease.

IN PRACTICE

Do you experience any of these physical symptoms? Take some time to write about the impact of C-PTSD on your health or medical history.

_____

_____

_____

_____

_____

_____

_____

_____

_____

_____

_____

_____

Looking Ahead

Here is what you can expect in this workbook. In chapter 2, we will explore the common methods used to treat C-PTSD, such as cognitive behavioral therapy, dialectical behavioral therapy, eye movement desensitization and reprocessing therapy, somatic psychotherapy, and mind-body perspectives. You will be introduced to the basic components of each model. These modalities provide the basis for the healing strategies you will learn in this workbook. The following three chapters will provide case studies that illustrate the major symptoms of C-PTSD and walk you through applicable treatment strategies. These will allow you to work through healing strategies that address each set of symptoms and focus on the ones that most affect you.

Chapter Takeaways

This chapter gave you an opportunity to deepen your understanding of C-PTSD and developmental trauma. Now, take a few minutes to check in with yourself. Look over your notes about any depressive, intrusive, and avoidance symptoms that may be present within your life. Likewise, explore how you feel as you review the physical symptoms of C-PTSD. With your increased knowledge of the links between stress, trauma, and emotional and physical health, what are you more aware of now? Use this space to express what you have learned.

2

Treating Complex PTSD

This chapter will help inform you about the various therapeutic approaches known to treat complex PTSD. There's no single therapy method that works best for healing C-PTSD. Therapists generally use a combination of psychotherapies that we will explore here, including CBT, DBT, EMDR therapy, somatic (body-centered) psychotherapy, and mindfulness—all administered within the context of a trusting relationship.

A workbook is not a replacement for psychotherapy. C-PTSD is relational trauma; in other words, it is harm caused by one person to another. There-fore, therapeutic interventions are most successful when you have a reliable rela-tionship with your therapist. If you are in the process of choosing a therapist, this information may help you choose the kind of therapist you would like to work with. In general, it is most important to choose someone that you feel is safe, trustworthy, compassionate, and understanding. Using this book as a supplement to therapy will allow you to empower yourself, be a more knowledgeable partner with your treat-ment providers, and more successfully achieve your health care goals.

> Healing asks that you turn toward your past to find relief from the weight of trauma. As a result, you become less defined by your history and have greater choice about your future.

The topic of C-PTSD can bring up vulnerable emotions. If anything starts to feel too painful or uncomfortable, you can always put this book down. Listen to your intuition about how to pace yourself. There is nothing wrong with slowing the process down if you need more time to integrate new information. Again, I strongly encourage you to seek out a qualified therapeutic professional, especially if you need more support than self-help can provide.

Cognitive Behavioral Therapy (CBT)

Originally developed by Dr. Aaron Beck in the 1960s, cognitive behavioral therapy (CBT) is still considered one of the most effective types of counseling for PTSD. In general, CBT helps you recognize the relationships between your thoughts, emotions, and behaviors. CBT assists in replacing distorted or distressing thoughts with more accurate and positive beliefs. Two forms of CBT are most frequently applied to the treatment of PTSD: exposure therapy and cognitive processing therapy.

EXPOSURE THERAPY

Exposure therapy involves desensitizing yourself to the trauma by repeatedly talking about your traumatic memories until you feel less overwhelmed by them. While initially it may feel uncomfortable to talk about the trauma, turning toward your past can be empowering. This method also employs relaxation methods and breathing exercises to calm down your mind and body. There has been concern that this method can sometimes be too direct, and as a result, feel re-traumatizing to some. It is important to trust your instincts when choosing the right therapy for you, and to speak up when a method feels uncomfortable or ineffective, so your therapist is aware and can help or change the process.

COGNITIVE PROCESSING THERAPY (CPT)

Cognitive processing therapy (CPT) reduces the power of fearful memories by activating a fearful memory while simultaneously introducing new information that is incompatible with beliefs surrounding the memory. For example, a belief that the trauma was your own fault is challenged when you recognize that you were just a child; you couldn't have done anything wrong. CPT educates about PTSD symptoms; helps develop awareness of your thoughts and feelings; guides you to incorporate new, more positive beliefs; and encourages practicing new skills that propel insights into actions.

NEGATIVE BELIEFS

All forms of CBT explore any inaccurate beliefs you may hold. Common negative beliefs include:

- I am unlovable
- I am unimportant
- I am unworthy
- I do not deserve to exist
- I don't belong
- I am helpless or powerless
- I cannot trust anyone
- I did something wrong

A key component of treatment is to replace negative self-statements with positive beliefs. Some examples include:

- I am lovable
- I am important
- I am worthy
- I survived

- I belong
- I am strong
- It is safe to love and trust now
- I can learn from my past

IN PRACTICE

Take a few minutes to look over the preceding list of negative beliefs. Which statements do you relate to, if any? Are there any other inaccurate beliefs that you tell yourself that are not listed here?

_____

_____

_____

_____

_____

_____

_____

What positive beliefs can you relate to? Write down some alternative beliefs. You can choose from the preceding list, or brainstorm any other positive statements that feel right for you.

_____

_____

_____

_____

_____

_____

_____

THE HEALING RELATIONSHIP

A core dilemma of C-PTSD is that your longing for connection conflicts with memories that tell you relationships aren't safe. It can be a challenge to develop healthy relationships. Initially, you may re-create relationships that match what you already know. Perhaps you unintentionally push people away and then feel angry that nobody ever calls you. Maybe you tend to choose partners who treat you poorly because deep inside this feels familiar.

In contrast, a healing relationship (such as one with a trusted therapist) will allow you to gently recognize and take responsibility for any part you may play in perpetuating unhealthy dynamics. In a trusting relationship, you can expose your fears and learn that you will not be rejected or harmed. Slowly, you'll learn to allow another person to witness your confusion, discomfort, anger, grief, or shame.

Even the healthiest of relationships have moments of disconnection or unintentional misunderstanding. A healing relationship will allow you to stay in the relationship until connection is regained and the relationship bond is repaired. Although nobody likes conflict, there is an intrinsic value in healthy conflict, for this process will actually help retrain your nervous system as you build trust in your capacity to successfully navigate through interpersonal challenges. Ultimately this process will help you form new relationship expectations that lead to healthier relationships in your life.

Dialectical Behavior Therapy (DBT)

Dialectical behavior therapy (DBT) was originally developed in the 1980s as a specific type of cognitive behavioral therapy for the treatment of borderline personality disorder. More recently, DBT has been applied to treat other disorders, and has been found particularly beneficial for C-PTSD. This therapy is founded on principles of Zen Buddhist philosophy and contemplative practices. For example, the term *dialectical* refers to a synthesis of opposites, which is a core aspect of Zen practices. The primary dialectic within DBT is the polarity between acceptance and change, which recognizes that radical acceptance of who you are is a necessary condition for change and growth. Typically, DBT therapy involves individual and/or group therapy sessions that focus on the development of mindfulness, emotion regulation, distress tolerance, and interpersonal effectiveness.

MINDFULNESS

Within the context of DBT, mindfulness skills focus on developing your capacity to observe your own mind while cultivating acceptance. Acceptance helps you recognize that uncomfortable experiences do not necessitate escape tactics or reactivity. DBT offers the concept of "Wise Mind," which represents the optimal balance of your "reasonable mind" (or thinking) with your "emotional mind" (or feeling)—an integration of logic and intuition that can help you feel calm and centered.

EMOTION REGULATION

DBT emotion regulation skills are based in a context of mindfulness and acceptance. The goal with this approach is not to get rid of your emotions; rather, it is to reduce suffering related to ineffective reactions to your emotions. An example would be lashing out at a supportive partner in fear or anger when perhaps they've done nothing wrong—this reaction causes additional suffering for you and your partner. DBT distinguishes that difficult feelings are not destructive or the result of a bad attitude. These emotions are simply meant to be felt, and this is where the mindfulness and acceptance come in. Emotion regulation helps you learn to distinguish between feelings and "action urges," which encourages you to reflect on your thoughts and emotions before jumping to reactions or behaviors.

DISTRESS TOLERANCE

Pain and distress are a basic part of life, and sadly, they cannot be entirely avoided. The goal of distress tolerance in DBT is to be able to handle painful emotions skillfully. Sometimes skillful action involves acceptance—welcoming reality as it is, without needing to resist or change it. Other times, skillful action requires change; such as recognizing when it is important to leave an unhealthy situation.

INTERPERSONAL EFFECTIVENESS

The DBT skills taught for interpersonal effectiveness emphasize assertiveness, boundaries, and coping with conflict. Assertiveness focuses on developing your capacity to ask for what you need, even though you may be told no or risk feeling rejected. Self-assertion involves building self-respect and cultivating a sense of your own worthiness. Skills for interpersonal effectiveness include learning to address conflicts gently, such as by refraining from put-downs or name-calling, respecting yourself and others, ensuring that you are behaving fairly, apologizing when you have done something wrong, and being truthful. These basic skills can be powerful catalysts for inner strength and positive self-esteem.

IN PRACTICE

Take a look at some common myths or misbeliefs about interpersonal effectiveness:

- I am weak if I make a mistake.
- I can't make a request unless I already know someone will say yes.
- If I ask for what I need, I am pushy (bad, selfish).
- Saying no is selfish.
- I automatically feel at fault if someone is angry with me.
- It is more important to sacrifice my own needs than say no.

Write down how you might challenge these beliefs with your own thoughts. What are some more helpful ways to look at them?

_____

_____

_____

_____

_____

_____

_____

GROUP THERAPY

Group therapy offers powerful benefits that individual therapy can't provide. Joining a group can be intimidating at first; however, the rewards tend to outweigh the risks. For example, talking about your trauma with others who have similar histories can help you feel more comfortable with your past and reduce your sense of isolation. You can develop relationships with others who understand what you have been through, and, in doing so, discover that you are not alone.

Sometimes it is important to have individual therapy prior to entering group therapy to be able to tolerate the vulnerability of sharing with others. It is also common to attend group and individual therapy simultaneously. There are two different kinds of groups: skills-based psychoeducation groups that focus on cultivating personal skills like mindfulness, distress tolerance, emotion regulation, and interpersonal relationship management; and process groups that use interaction with other attendees to provide opportunities to establish trust, give and receive feedback, and work through conflicts in real time.

The truth is, we all need each other to heal relationship wounds. Unfortunately, our culture has a collective blind spot when it comes to vulnerable emotions—this stigma exists even in healthy homes. You may have been taught to minimize your pain, to pretend you were fine when you weren't, or to gloss over feelings. In order to heal, it is important to release your conditioned hiding, and to recognize that others share your longing for authentic presence. Therapy groups provide a safe container for opening up and healing in a community setting.

EMDR Therapy

Eye movement desensitization and reprocessing (EMDR) therapy, developed by Dr. Francine Shapiro, is a comprehensive approach to therapy that integrates elements of several different therapies. EMDR therapy is structured to treat PTSD by identifying triggering memories, emotions, beliefs, and sensations. It relies on the concept that with sufficient support, you'll have the capacity to process and digest traumatic events. As a result, you'll be able to let go of self-critical beliefs and painful emotions.

EIGHT PHASE TREATMENT MODEL

EMDR therapy uses a treatment model split into eight phases. The initial phases prepare you to process the trauma by identifying traumatic memories and the negative beliefs associated with them. You then review your history by taking an in-depth look at your symptoms. For example, feelings of insecurity are understood to be symptoms that are rooted in historical experiences. The desensitization phase incorporates the use of a dual awareness state, in which you are asked to remain aware of your present moment experience while simultaneously recalling memories of the traumatic event. Dual attention is amplified using stimulation in the form of eye movements, buzzers, or tones that alternate between the left and right side of your body. Later phases of EMDR therapy focus on strengthening positive beliefs.

RESOURCES FOR EMDR THERAPY–BASED TRAUMA RECOVERY

The preparatory phase of EMDR therapy involves building resources to be able to attend to the frightening and sometimes overwhelming trauma-related memories. These resources include:

- **Safe place:** Here you identify a place that is either real or imaginary, and where you feel safe, allowing your body and mind to have a reference place that supports relaxation and ease.

- **Containment:** Here you develop an imagined container: a place or item that is big and strong enough to hold painful thoughts, feelings, and memories. The container is meant to be used temporarily during times when you are not actively engaged in processing your traumatic memories.
- **Allies:** Here you identify imagined or real beings that you associate with nurturance, protection, and wisdom. Allies can be people, animals, or spiritual or religious figures.

FUTURE INSTALLATION

EMDR therapy not only processes past events, but also identifies the necessary positive beliefs to facilitate greater choice in the present. For example, once an individual no longer holds the misconception that they are unlovable, they can begin to develop and integrate a new positive belief that they are worthy of being loved.

IN PRACTICE

Visualizing a safe or peaceful place is a primary resource, because that safe place will best allow your body and mind to release the effects of stress and trauma. Think of a place that evokes a feeling of safety and peace. Your place can be a real place you have been, a scene from a movie, or something entirely imagined. Some people choose favorite settings in nature, such as sitting near the ocean or by a stream. Some choose to think about a pet or a loved one. The main consideration when developing safe place imagery is that it truly feels safe for you. Here you can use your senses to enhance your imagery. What do you see? What do you hear? What are the smells?

When creating a safe place image, you may notice the need for refinements—that is, your thoughts can get in the way. For example, one woman's peaceful place was in a wildflower meadow. During her visualization, a lion entered the scene, interrupting her feeling of safety. When disruptions happen in your safe place, it is actually a signal to create reinforcements to strengthen your feeling of safety. In her case, we added a wall around the meadow and placed guards to ensure that no invaders could enter the meadow. You can enhance your own visualization by adding protectors, bringing in nurturing people, or placing animals that act as allies in your imagined safe place.

Take a few moments to write down your safe place visualization. It is helpful to imagine your safe place on a regular basis to strengthen your ability to connect to this positive feeling as needed.

_____

_____

_____

_____

_____

_____

_____

_____

_____

Somatic Psychotherapy

Somatic modalities are therapy approaches that focus on the body rather than the mind. Therapies such as Somatic Experiencing® (developed by Peter Levine) and Sensorimotor Psychotherapy (developed by Pat Ogden) engage body awareness to release the psychological and physiological impact of traumatic events. Reasoning and logic alone are seldom sufficient to treat trauma. When exposed to frightening experiences, your breath quickens and tension builds throughout your body. To process trauma, you need to breathe and move. However, our culture tends toward stillness in the face of trauma. When body awareness is not included in trauma processing, you inhibit your ability to work with your innate healing capacities. Somatic awareness, or an awareness of your body's sensations, can teach you how to gauge your body's feedback so you can recognize when your traumatic past no longer holds power over you.

SOMATIC AWARENESS

Somatic psychotherapists invite clients to be curious about body sensations. Mindfully staying connected to the body in the midst of powerful emotions or sensations helps clients regulate and respond more effectively to emotional intensity. Simply bringing awareness to physical tension and breath patterns begins the process of healing.

SEQUENCING

Sequencing refers to the movement of tension out from the core of your body through the extremities. It can be involuntary, but can also be facilitated through mindful movements such as following an urge to move something. Sequencing is helpful, as it allows the releasing of tension patterns related to freeze, fight, or flight responses in the body. Sometimes sequencing occurs as a visible trembling in the arms or legs. Other times it is experienced as a movement pattern as seen in Julie's story:

Julie had a history of childhood sexual abuse. As she discussed her past, she felt an impulse to crouch and bend over. Mindfully she curled into a tight ball as if she were hiding. After several minutes, she felt a desire to push her arms out and kick her legs. She slowly engaged in these self-protective movements. Once she returned to stillness, she described a new feeling in her body that was both empowered and calm.

GROUNDING

Grounding refers to your ability to sense your body, feel your feet on the earth, and as a result, calm your nervous system. This concept sits at the heart of somatic psychotherapies. Grounding is a key resource for trauma and emotional overwhelm. Your senses (hearing, seeing, smelling, tasting, touching) are tools for anchoring yourself in the present moment.

WORKING WITH PARTS

Treating complex PTSD often involves "parts work" as a way to understand avoidance, intrusive, and depressive symptoms. Often referred to as ego state therapy, this approach to healing recognizes that you develop different parts of yourself to hold unwanted or unacceptable feelings and memories. Ego states are often parts that reflect younger developmental phases of your life related to traumatic memories. This is why you might sometimes feel like a wounded child or a rebellious teenager. Parts can also represent an internalization from your family of origin. For instance, you can think of an inner critic as an internalization of a critical parent from childhood.

While many therapies work with parts in the healing process, let's take a closer look at Internal Family Systems (IFS) therapy, which was developed by Dr. Richard Schwartz. He identified three kinds of parts:

- **Exiles:** Exiles carry the burdens of trauma. They are the parts of yourself that you cut off from conscious awareness as a way to distance yourself from painful memories and emotions such as rage, dependency, shame, fear, loneliness, or grief. Often these parts feel young.

- **Managers:** Managers attempt to protect you from vulnerable feelings by staying in control. They tend to be overly rigid and self-critical or rely heavily upon prescribed roles such as planning or caretaking.

- **Firefighters:** Firefighters act out in order to repress exiles as they attempt to emerge. This part employs substances, self-harm, or dissociation to distract you from your underlying emotional vulnerability.

The goal of IFS therapy is to develop your relationship to the Self, which Dr. Schwartz describes as the core of who you are. When you are living from this center, you have the capacity to be calm, confident, and compassionate. The Self is your own source of wisdom or inner knowing. When you reside in the Self, you are able to regulate the other parts of you, allowing for an internal felt sense of trust, harmony, and connection.

IN PRACTICE

A body scan is an essential tool that helps you develop somatic awareness. Explore this guided practice:

- Find a comfortable seated position on a chair or cushion that you can maintain for the next several minutes. The aim of this practice is to cultivate awareness of your body without judgment. As you read each set of instructions, take a moment to tune into each area of your body, increasing your awareness of your sensations and the experience.
- First, bring your attention to your breath. Make space for whatever you are feeling, including any areas of tension, heaviness, or constriction.
- Now, bring your awareness to your feet, legs, and pelvis. Notice the sensations in your muscles and on your skin.
- Next, take a deep breath as you bring your attention into your torso, becoming aware of any sensations in your abdomen and lower back. Notice your spine and any sensations across your chest or upper back.
- Now, bring your awareness to your shoulders, arms, and hands. Notice any areas of tension or relaxation.
- Last, bring your attention to your neck, throat, and face. Notice your eyes, your mouth, and your tongue and the general sensations of your head.
- As you complete your body scan, take a final moment to notice your body as a whole.
- Write down some notes about your experience.
- The body scan initially functions to help increase your awareness of your body's tension patterns. With this awareness as a foundation, you can choose to deepen your curiosity about your sensations, or use relaxation techniques to release holding.
- For example, if you notice tension in your shoulders, you might amplify the sensations by lifting your shoulders a little higher toward your ears. Squeeze your shoulders up, and notice how you feel as you increase the tension. What emotions arise? What thoughts are you aware of? Next, consciously let your shoulders go. Notice the contrast. What are you aware of now?

It is helpful to repeat the body scan regularly to strengthen your body awareness as a guide for healing.

_____

_____

_____

_____

_____

_____

_____

_____

_____

_____

_____

_____

_____

_____

_____

_____

Complementary and Alternative Medicine (CAM)

Complementary and alternative medicine (CAM) interventions, such as relaxation, mindfulness, and yoga, have been integrated into many mental health centers and hospitals as supportive treatment for PTSD. They work by regulating your autonomic nervous system (ANS). Recall that your ANS consists of sympathetic and parasympathetic nervous system states. Optimally, you can reclaim balance in your body and mind by finding ways to calm down when anxious and feel nurtured by your capacity to rest and feel nourished. However, with C-PTSD it is common to react to situations in ways that can be irrational, or not

POSITIVE PSYCHOLOGY AND RESILIENCE

Positive psychology focuses on strengths and capabilities rather than diagnoses or deficits. In treating PTSD, applying the science of positive psychology recognizes that you have the ability to be resilient despite your traumatic history. You can adapt well and even be strengthened by adversity. For example, many people who have traumatic histories report having a strengthened commitment to happiness and a life path with purpose and determination.

Resilience is not a trait that you either have or do not have. It is a set of strategies that can be learned and practiced by anyone. Strategies include:

- Cultivating a growth mind-set, in which you believe you can grow through both positive and negative life events
- Staying connected to your community rather than isolating yourself
- Successfully working through difficult emotions
- Believing that you have the capacity to shape the course of your life now
- Supporting your physical health through movement and exercise
- Expressing yourself through journaling and creativity

Resilience is a process that is best served when you actively participate in supporting your physical, mental, emotional, social, and spiritual health each and every day. You can build your resilience by engaging in small actions such as calling a friend, writing for five minutes in your journal, or taking a walk around the block. While each one of these steps might seem small, collectively they can help you feel strong, relaxed, capable, and more connected to others in the world. The practices offered in this workbook are aimed at developing your resilience and strengthening your positive mind-set.

based in reality. In such moments, feelings of worry, frustration, or hopelessness can interfere with your ability to take care of yourself and your relationships in healthy ways.

Mary came into therapy sharing that she struggles with feelings of insecurity and lack of trust. She explained that during the day, she will often text or call her boyfriend. She stated that she knows he is at work, is busy, and doesn't have time to check his phone. However, she just can't relax. She begins to feel anxious and starts to believe that he has plans to leave her for another woman. As her anxiety builds, she feels angry and abandoned. Sometimes she gets so worked up that she will call and text repeatedly until he finally answers, reassuring her of his love. But if she doesn't get a call back, she eventually shuts down, numbing herself with TV until he gets home. At that point she feels so hurt and resentful that she inadvertently pushes him away.

Mary's experience reveals a common trajectory of how feelings of abandonment, anxiety, and exhaustion can take over when we don't have the tools to remain calm and mindful. Let's take a closer look at the science behind this downward spiral:

The *vagus nerve* plays a central role in ANS regulation because it connects your brain to your digestive system, heart, lungs, throat, and facial muscles. Dr. Stephen Porges introduced *polyvagal theory*, which proposes your nervous system reflects a developmental progression with three evolutionary stages:

- When you experience a stressful event, your ANS responds with sympathetic nervous system mobilization into the fight-or-flight response. This process aims to protect you and help you reestablish safety.
- If you can't resolve the stressful situation or are facing a life-threatening event, you will resort to an earlier set of evolutionary mechanisms maintained by the *dorsal vagal complex* (DVC). This parasympathetic branch of your vagus nerve puts an abrupt, unrefined brake on your sympathetic nervous system by promoting immobilizing defensive actions such as fatigue, depression, or dissociation—consider concepts like fainting or feigning death.

- In order to regulate your ANS, you need to engage the most recently evolved parasympathetic branch of the vagus nerve called the *ventral vagal complex* (VVC), or alternatively, the social nervous system. This branch functions as a highly refined brake on sympathetic activation, and has a calming and soothing effect.

Importantly, both the DVC and VVC have parasympathetic actions that exert inhibition on the sympathetic nervous system. The DVC inhibits it in a negative way (dissociation, helplessness, and despair), which can have serious repercussions on mental and physical health. Conversely, the VVC is associated with increases in health and emotional well-being, as it allows you to rest, digest, and relax into feelings of safety and connection.

You can better understand this process by thinking of a young toddler separated from a primary caregiver. Initially the child will cry and cling, as is typical with separation anxiety. If the child is reconnected with the caregiver or soothed by another adult, the distress will eventually resolve and the child will rest or play. However, what if the child cries without any caring response or reconnection? Perhaps the child will develop a capacity to self-soothe, but if that doesn't happen, the distress will continue. When screaming and crying produce no sense of reconnection and safety, the child might eventually collapse into helplessness or fall asleep from fatigue.

Your social nervous system is strengthened by repeated practice. Ideally, this practice occurred in early childhood with a loving and consistent caregiver. However, with situations of early neglect or abuse, this was not the case. It is essential to develop your social nervous system in other ways. This can occur within healthy relationships in adulthood such as with a psychotherapist. CAM therapies such as relaxation, mindfulness practices, tai chi, qigong, and yoga all strengthen the social nervous system.

RELAXATION TECHNIQUES

Relaxation techniques are beneficial for the healing of C-PTSD. Some of the most common and well-researched techniques include progressive muscle relaxation (PMR), visualization, and diaphragmatic breathing. In each of these practices, you focus on calming down your body. In PMR, you sequentially tense and relax various muscle groups (e.g., arms, legs, torso, neck) throughout your entire body. Visualization involves recalling memories of times when you felt relaxed, and allowing your body to respond accordingly. Slow and rhythmic diaphragmatic breathing, or "belly breathing," helps calm you down if your body is in a fight-or-flight response.

MINDFULNESS

Mindfulness in psychotherapy involves engaging in practices that encourage awareness of the present moment, a mind-set of nonjudgment, focus on bodily felt senses, relaxation techniques, and awareness of breathing patterns. Mindfulness has many proven benefits for mental and physical health. Two well-known programs include mindfulness-based stress reduction (MBSR), developed by Dr. Jon Kabat-Zinn, to manage stress and anxiety, and mindfulness-based cognitive therapy (MBCT), developed by Dr. Zindel Segal and colleagues, which applies mindfulness to treat major depressive disorder. Research on the effectiveness of mindfulness practices reveals improvements in anxiety, depression, sleep disorders, asthma, chronic pain, fibromyalgia, heart disease, gastrointestinal diseases, and diabetes.

> Resilience is not a trait that you either have or do not have. It is a set of strategies that can be learned and practiced by anyone.

THERAPEUTIC YOGA

Yoga is not a stretching practice. It is an opportunity to explore physical postures within a context of mindfulness, conscious breathing, and somatic (body) awareness. You go into this with an intention to become aware of your moment-to-moment experience while cultivating self-compassion. Therapeutic yoga is less interested in the outer look of a pose, which can be a disservice if you have self-critical or perfectionist tendencies. Instead, key components of a therapeutic yoga practice include supplying yourself with an environment that feels emotionally and physically safe, minimizing the use of mirrors, and setting a tone of gentleness and nonjudgment.

> One woman's safe place was her grandmother's kitchen. She could see the wallpaper, the light coming through the window. She remembered how they talked and laughed while she and her grandmother made cookies. She imagined the smell of the cookies in the oven. All of this brought this relaxing memory back to life, allowing her to feel safe and peaceful in the present moment.

Research is also showing benefits of the trauma-sensitive yoga program in the treatment of PTSD. This treatment model includes attendance at a trauma-sensitive yoga class as a supplementary treatment alongside psychotherapy for PTSD. The physical practice of yoga offers opportunities to explore strength-building by assuming standing postures such as warrior pose or downward dog. Restorative postures such as child's pose provide a complementary action by practicing the art of surrender and letting go. Attending a yoga class has added benefits, including developing a sense of community and reducing the feelings of isolation associated with PTSD.

IN PRACTICE

Controlling breath is one of the fastest ways to regulate your nervous system. The aim of this breath practice is to slow down the pace of your breath to relax and calm your body and mind. This practice involves an equal count for the

THE FIVE MINDFULNESS MYTHS

There are common myths and misconceptions that can lead some to feel reticent to participate in this valuable healing tool. Let's take a closer look by deconstructing the common mindfulness myths:

- **Myth 1: Mindfulness is about religion.** You do not need to be a Buddhist to be mindful. Mindfulness is a human practice of curiosity and nonjudgmental self-observation that can be practiced by anyone.

- **Myth 2: Mindfulness is meditation.** While meditation offers the opportunity to practice being mindful, the two are not necessarily synonymous. The aim of mindfulness is to remain aware anywhere. You can explore being mindful while eating, doing the dishes, talking a walk, or engaging in conversation.

- **Myth 3: Mindfulness is about enlightenment.** Being mindful is not about becoming smarter, better, or superhuman. Mindfulness is often deeply humbling as you develop your capacity to honestly reflect upon your own humanness and the simple things around you that you might never have noticed before.

- **Myth 4: Mindfulness is relaxing.** Sometimes but not always. Simply paying attention can increase your awareness of turbulent emotions or conflicts that perhaps you were avoiding. However, mindfulness can also give you the tools to work more consciously with difficult experiences.

- **Myth 5: Mindfulness is about self-improvement.** It is normal to become distracted during a mindfulness practice. Rather than becoming frustrated with yourself, practice gently inviting your attention back to your breath and the present moment.

inhale and the exhale. Start with a count of 4; you can lengthen this count as you become comfortable with the practice.

Find a comfortable seated position. This can be in a chair or a cushion on the floor; whatever allows you to sit comfortably for the next several minutes. Take a few moments to notice your physical sensations. Do you notice any areas of tension? Are there any areas that feel more relaxed or at ease? Now, inhale slowly through your nose for a count of 4, and exhale slowly for a count of 4. Continue this breath cycle for the next 2 minutes. Notice the changes in your body and the mind in response to your rhythmic, balanced breathing. Over time, you might be able to increase the length of time of your practice to 5 minutes or longer.

What do you notice as a result of this breathing practice? Write down some notes about your experience. Repeat this practice as needed.

_____

_____

_____

_____

_____

_____

_____

_____

_____

_____

_____

_____

_____

_____

_____

_____

OTHER TREATMENTS FOR C-PTSD

Many other therapeutic modalities offer beneficial perspectives for the healing of C-PTSD. While not all can be discussed in depth, a few remain noteworthy:

- **Acceptance and commitment therapy (ACT):** Developed by Dr. Steven Hayes, ACT is a form of cognitive behavioral therapy that uses acceptance and mindfulness strategies to increase what is known as *psychological flexibility*, your capacity to live in the present moment with wisely chosen behaviors. ACT uses metaphors to support healing. For example, saying "emotions are like the weather" invites you to take a mindful walk to determine the current forecast of your feelings. Is today calm with a few sun showers, or are you facing a raging tornado? How might you prepare for either situation? Such a practice might allow you to notice your need to attend to feelings of vulnerability, in which case you might add in a mindful walk or a journaling practice before going to work in the morning.

- **Narrative exposure therapy (NET):** NET is a specific treatment for all trauma disorders, including complex PTSD. Here you identify significant events, which are deemed "flowers and stones" within the context of your life story. Flowers are the positive events, such as loving people or personal accomplishments. Stones are your difficult or traumatic life events. The aim of this therapy is to be able to develop a complete biographical narrative, inclusive of both stones and flowers, to strengthen your sense of personal identity.

- **Neurofeedback:** Neurofeedback uses EEG monitoring to improve brain functioning as you learn to alter your brain activity. By using computer imaging, you receive direct feedback through a "brain map" that indicates areas of your brain with excessive activity associated with PTSD, such as your fear centers. Here you learn how to relax your body and mind to activate the outermost layer of your brain; that which is associated with thinking and decision-making. Typically, 20 sessions will give you enough feedback to understand how to facilitate regulation of your body and mind on your own.

Bumps in the Road

No therapeutic process is without its challenges and pitfalls, but if you are pre-pared for them, you can better address them when they occur. Let's look at some of the common difficulties that can arise during therapy so you can carefully navi-gate these bumps in the road.

OVERWHELM

You might notice an increase in distressing symptoms as you begin to "look at" instead of "look away from" your difficult past—these are temporary. It can be helpful to think of these symptoms as a sign that you are actually moving in the right direction. Remember that attending to your past will ultimately bring you great benefits. However, when too many distressing symptoms come up at once, healing can be compromised. It is possible to feel re-traumatized if you feel flooded or overwhelmed. You can manage the intensity by slowing down the pace of how and when you attend to trauma-related memories. You can also strengthen your connection to positive resources, such as supportive friends or relaxation techniques, as a way to manage overwhelm.

RESISTANCE

It is common and natural to want to push away from the healing process. Get-ting close to traumatic material can feel threatening. You might want to put this book down and not read any more. If you are currently in therapy, you might feel a desire to cancel appointments or fail to show up. Therapeutic resistance is one form of avoidance you might try in order to protect yourself from pain. Despite your longing to heal, you may start running the other way. Some examples of resistance include lying to yourself or your therapist, feeling impatient or angry with the pace of therapy, being discouraged about your healing, or feeling bored with therapy. However, resistance can sabotage the healing experience. The good news is that if you are encountering resistance in therapy, you are likely on the right track. Be sure to share these resistant or negative feelings with your therapist, who will be able to support you. As you face what you have been avoiding, you will eventually feel better and perhaps even empowered for tackling one of the roadblocks to healing.

UNHEALTHY URGES

Another form of resistance in psychotherapy is a desire to turn toward addictive habits such as emotional eating, drinking, or using drugs. Addictions are another way of avoiding pain. As you reflect upon traumatic memories, you might find an increase in urges to use, or to numb yourself to get away from the pain. You can deal with addictive habits by deepening your understanding of what you are trying to avoid and countering the habits by developing more positive coping behaviors. Discuss these behaviors with your therapist and know that as you broaden your capacity to tolerate difficult emotions, your addictive behaviors will likely decrease.

PERFECTIONISM

Therapy is messy and often uncomfortable. In order to heal, it is necessary to let go of any need you might have to manage how other people see you. If you are like most people, you prefer to be seen as strong, capable, intelligent, and in control. However, it is important to recognize that nobody feels like this all of the time. Bringing the true you—even the messy, hidden parts of yourself—into the therapy room is an important step toward healing. This can involve taking off the masks that you might wear to protect yourself in your daily life and a willingness to accept your imperfections with self-compassion and nonjudgment.

Look over the preceding common defense strategies that can arise during therapy. In what ways can you relate? In what ways could you see overwhelm, resistance, unhealthy urges, or perfectionism interfering with your healing process?

_____

_____

_____

_____

_____

Am I Ready for Treatment?

To successfully heal from C-PTSD, you need to feel safe and stable in your life now. For example, living in an unsafe environment or having an active addiction will get in the way of your healing. Even positive changes such as moving into a new house or having a new baby can be destabilizing. Reading and writing about difficult life events can bring up disturbing emotions. It will be important that you have sufficient resources in order to heal. Use this checklist to determine if this is the right time for you to work through your trauma and to ensure that you have what you need, emotionally and physically, to heal.

The following readiness questions are based on guidelines from *Trauma-Informed Care in Behavioral Health Services*, published by the Substance Abuse and Mental Health Services Administration, part of the US Department of Health and Human Services. If your answer is yes to any of the following questions, discuss your answers with a therapist or other health care provider so you can work together to develop an appropriate approach for you:

- Is there any current life change or crisis that might interfere with your healing at this time?
- Do you feel unsafe or unstable now within your living environment or relationship?

- Have you faced any recent traumatic events that are interfering with stability in your life?
- Are you dealing with any significant illness or physical health crisis?
- Have you recently engaged in self-harm/cutting behaviors?
- Have you had a recent suicide plan or attempt?
- Do you have severe dissociative symptoms including periods of numbness, feeling like you are not living your own life, "lost time," or lapses in memory?
- Do you have an active, untreated eating disorder?
- Are you using drugs or alcohol to excess?
- If you are sober, do you have less than a year of sobriety, which may put you at greater risk of relapse?
- Are you lacking necessary stabilizing resources (therapist, psychiatrist, access to health care, sponsor if needed)?

A Roadmap to Healing

Most trauma treatment specialists, including clinical psychiatrist and trauma expert Dr. Judith Herman, view healing and recovery as occurring in three phases. Let's look more closely at these phases of healing, which are applicable to any of the therapies mentioned in this book:

- **Phase I:** The main work of this phase is to develop stability and safety. Here you will learn to identify your defensive avoidance behaviors and develop mindfulness practices that are instrumental for self-acceptance and compassion. You'll develop instrumental resources to help you prepare for trauma processing.
- **Phase II:** Within this phase, you will continue to strengthen your resources to manage intrusive or invasive symptoms of C-PTSD. You will increase your ability to regulate emotions and tolerate distress, and you'll deepen your understanding of your history. The main work of this stage is to process trauma memories in a way that lessens your emotional intensity and brings an increased sense of personal liberation from the past.

- **Phase III:** Within this phase, you will attend to depressive symptoms by increasing your understanding of shame and helplessness as they relate to C-PTSD. You'll work through grief related to your childhood experiences. The main work of this phase is to integrate your unique life events into a positive sense of self.

The next three chapters walk you through these phases of healing. Know that the healing journey is not necessarily linear—the steps tend to occur in more of a spiral fashion. For instance, when you're feeling overwhelmed in Phase II, you can touch back on Phase I for greater stabilization. Rather than trying to race to the finish line, be like the tortoise; walk the healing path slow and steady.

Chapter Takeaways

This chapter introduced you to the most common modalities used by therapists to treat C-PTSD. The intention is to inform you of the breadth of therapies available and to help you find the right balance between self-healing and therapy. Using this book as a supplement to therapy will allow you to empower yourself by partnering with your treatment providers.

Take a few minutes to review your notes within the In Practice sections of this chapter. What are the negative beliefs that resonated with you? In what ways did you challenge the common myths about interpersonal effectiveness? What was the safe place you identified? Have you been able to connect to that place on a regular basis? How did you feel during the body scan and the breathing practices? Finally, what possible bumps in the road do you anticipate as you progress through this workbook?

_____

_____

_____

_____

_____

_____

Now take a few minutes to check in with yourself. What are you aware of now? Use this space to explore what you have learned.

3

Renee's Story
Healing Avoidance Symptoms

When Renee and I first met, she was reluctant to tell me about her life. She felt embarrassed and ashamed. Once she recognized that I was not there to judge her, she slowly began to share how difficult things had become. She spoke of her anxiety and anger. A stay-at-home mother of two young children, Renee said that she's trying not to take her frustration out on the kids, but she is yelling more than she would like to admit: "I promised myself I would parent differently than I was raised, but I find myself saying the exact things my mother used to say." As a result, she said, she hates herself even more.

Renee shared that she has started to fantasize about running away, and that she sometimes believes her children would be better off without her. She has withdrawn from her husband, who has said he feels like he doesn't know her anymore. She copes with food; eating junk food during the day and having a drink or two in the evenings deadens the pain. She said, "I'm afraid I'm ruining my kids and pushing my husband so far away that he will leave. But I guess he still loves me; he was the one who finally urged me to come into therapy."

Renee spent many years pushing away her difficult past. However, becoming a parent has brought to the surface feelings and memories about how Renee was raised by her mother. She began relying upon avoidance strategies of emotional eating and drinking alcohol to "hold herself together." This maladaptive way of coping was no longer working.

Renee's story is just one example of feeling trapped by symptoms of complex PTSD. It is common to not be able to see a way out. Relationships, work, or children can feel like "too much," and as a result, it is easy to fall into patterns of withdrawal from life. This chapter provides resources for the symptoms of avoidance. These include denying your past, repressing feelings, minimizing your distress, or numbing the pain with substances.

Through multiple therapeutic perspectives, you will learn valuable ways to soften your defenses so you can turn toward the difficult events of your past.

The goal of this phase of trauma treatment is to develop enough stabilization of your symptoms so you can address your traumatic memories without becoming overwhelmed or flooded.

Avoidance and Defenses

Avoidance behaviors come in many forms and are upheld by psychological defenses. You may have developed strong walls around your most vulnerable feelings. Maybe you use emotional eating, drinking, or excessive exercising. Perhaps you resist going out places or seeing people. These protective maneuvers come with unwanted consequences, such as physical health impairments or loss of relationships that leave you feeling isolated. This section

> **Resistance is information, and your job is to become curious enough to understand the message.**

will help you identify your defenses so you can create changes that will address the underlying issues and resolve the need for such defenses. Let's take a closer look at some of the common psychological defenses:

- **Repression and denial:** You might bury painful feelings or thoughts away from your conscious awareness. "If I don't talk about or acknowledge my painful past, it doesn't exist."
- **Regression:** You might feel or act younger than you actually are as a way to avoid taking responsibility for your feelings and actions now. "If I just stay in bed and sleep all day, I don't have to go to work."
- **Idealization:** You might exaggerate the positive traits of your abusive caregiver rather than acknowledge how damaging this relationship was. In this case, the anger you feel can be misdirected toward yourself; for example, thinking, "If only I hadn't been so bad, I wouldn't have been locked in the basement." Idealization is often paired with devaluation—a polarized view in which people are either all good or all bad.
- **Fantasy:** You might engage in daydreaming about how things should be, or how you'd like them to be, rather than addressing challenges head-on. "It would be easier to run away than to get help with my anger."

- **Intellectualization:** You might avoid feelings by resorting to thinking or analyzing situations. Sometimes this defense structure underlies workaholism, in which you busy yourself with work to distract yourself from dealing with relationships or emotional pain. "I can think my way out of any challenge."
- **Projection:** You might assume that someone else is thinking or feeling in a way that actually reflects your own thoughts and feelings. For example, you feel sure your friend is angry with you, but you are in denial that it is actually you who is angry with your friend.
- **Dissociation:** You might separate the part of you that keeps up with daily tasks of living from scary or painful emotions and memories. Dissociation exists on a continuum from relatively mild sensations of fogginess, sleepiness, or difficulty concentrating to feeling numb or cut off. In the most extreme situations, you might have lapses of memory or "lost time."
- **Addictions:** It is common to use substances or maintain other addictive behaviors such as emotional eating or excessive exercising to avoid feeling pain. Here you might say, "Why *feel* anything when I can . . . eat, run, drink, smoke pot, take a Valium, etc."

IN PRACTICE

It can be hard to see your own defenses clearly or to be fully honest with yourself about behaviors that are no longer serving you. The truth is, we all employ defenses at some point in our lives. See if you can bring self-compassion to this process. Take a few minutes to look over the previous list of avoidance defenses.

Do you relate to any of these ways of pushing painful emotions or memories away?

_____

_____

_____

_____

_____

THE MEANING BEHIND RESISTANCE

"It is a joy to be hidden and disaster not to be found."
—D. W. Winnicott, pediatrician and psychoanalyst

The idea of resistance or defenses can be misinterpreted as being in the wrong. Within psychotherapy, clients who are referred to as "resistant" might be told that they are defiant, stubborn, or obstinate. This can result in a lack of trust in therapy.

I invite you to think of resistance as normal, healthy, and important. Resistance is information, and your job is to become curious enough to understand the message. This process requires compassion for yourself and from your therapist. If you have been told you are a "resistant client," it is important to understand what dynamics might be at play. Let's take a closer look at what resistance might be telling you:

- **Resistance can indicate good therapy:** Resistance can arise because therapy is going well. You are getting closer to painful memories and difficult feelings. You may backpedal as an attempt to slow down the therapy. In this situation, you and your therapist can check in about the pacing of therapy to ensure that you are not getting flooded or overwhelmed. In this case, you can focus on resource development and creating greater safety.

- **Resistance is a sign of ambivalence:** It is normal to have mixed feelings about change. Part of you may want to change, while another part may feel threatened or frightened. In this case, you can explore with your therapist any misgivings you have about letting go of your defenses and work through them together.

- **Resistance is a remnant of untrustworthy care:** If you have a history of misdiagnosis or feeling criticized by health care providers, you might feel reticent to talk openly or honestly about your internal struggles. If you have had a poor therapy experience in the past, it is understandable that you would feel tentative as you return or feel the need to test out the approach of your new therapist. In this case, it can be helpful to seek a referral from a friend, health care provider, or other trusted source, or investigate therapy resource websites to find a therapist whose philosophy resonates with you.

- **Resistance can be a sign of bad therapy:** Until you feel safe, you will not let go of your avoidance strategies. If you feel that your therapist lacks empathy, if you feel blamed, or if you are locked in a power struggle, it is impossible to feel safe. In this case, your "resistance" may actually be a sign that you need a therapist who takes a different approach. Complex PTSD is relationally based trauma; therefore, it is integral to treatment that you work with a therapist you can trust.

Defenses as Self-Protection

Renee recognized that she was pushing her husband and children away so that she didn't have to feel her own pain. As we explored her history, she told me her father had left her mother when Renee was only two years old. She described her mother as unavailable, but when she did pay attention to Renee, she was mean and sometimes physically abusive. As a child, Renee coped by fantasizing about running away; she would "go away" in her mind. Parenting two young children was triggering Renee's childhood memories, and she did not have sufficient resources to handle these feelings.

All defenses are learned behaviors. You only develop psychological defenses because they were once necessary for self-protection. In order to heal, it is important to become curious about your behaviors and their origins. The practice of being curious helps you cultivate insight, a deeper understanding that leads to compassion and acceptance.

In this case, you want to cultivate curiosity about the origin of your self-protective or defensive behaviors. Where or when might you have learned to stop allowing yourself to feel vulnerable? When did you learn to push away pain, or turn toward addictive substances? Do you recall a time when perhaps you decided to stop talking to people about your emotions, thoughts, hopes, or dreams? When did you learn, perhaps, that focusing on work helped to push your feelings away? If you can identify with any of these issues, recognize that you were doing the best you could to survive with the resources that you had at the time—and now, with self-awareness, you can change the way you handle these things.

> **"I have no special talents. I am only passionately curious."**
> —ALBERT EINSTEIN, physicist

IN PRACTICE

What connections are you making between your defenses and your past?
Use these lines to write about your experience and your thoughts.

_____

_____

_____

_____

_____

ACCEPTANCE AND CHANGE

Dr. Carl Rogers's classic psychology book, *On Becoming a Person*, starts with a personal reflection in which he writes, "The curious paradox is that when I accept myself just as I am, then I can change." It can feel threatening to give up strategies that helped you survive. Here is a simple story that offers a powerful metaphor about the role of acceptance in change:

The wind and the sun are looking below them at a man walking along a path wearing his jacket and scarf. The wind says to the sun, "I bet you that I can get the man to take off his jacket faster than you can!" Agreeing to the bet, the sun sits back and watches the wind blow and blow. The wind blows harder and harder, but in response, the man only buttons up his jacket and wraps his scarf tightly around him. The wind is unsuccessful; now it is the sun's turn. The sun shines brightly, and within minutes the man loosens his scarf, unbuttons his coat, and soon removes them both.

Notice how the sun represents warmth and acceptance, while the wind exemplifies a more aggressive approach to self-change, which often back-fires, leading us to cling more strongly to our defenses. In what ways are you holding tight to your protective defenses? In what way could kindness, warmth, or self-acceptance allow you to let go of your defenses and open you up to changing patterns that no longer serve you?

Radical Self-Acceptance

Renee had a hard time accepting herself. She was filled with judgment and shame about her behaviors. I suggested that it was important to develop a capacity to turn toward herself lovingly. At first she only felt disgust and anger, with statements like, "How could I love myself for yelling at my kids? Why should I deserve love? Look how fat and ugly I've become!" Renee was suffering so much that she decided to try something new. She began to integrate self-acceptance and mindfulness practices into her daily routine. She began journaling about her critical thought patterns; she explored new, positive ways of thinking about herself. As Renee softened her judgmental stance, she became aware of how lonely and scared she feels sometimes. She had access to a new sense of kindness and compassion for herself.

Dialectical behavioral therapy suggests that acceptance of who you are is a necessary condition for change and growth. Likewise, Buddhist psychologist Dr. Tara Brach encourages you to become your own best friend by employing radical self-acceptance and befriending your body. Let's take a closer look at how to incorporate practices that facilitate self-acceptance.

BREATH AWARENESS

Accepting reality as it is involves anchoring your mind in the sensations of your body. Observing your breath provides one way to focus your attention into a present-moment experience of your body. Notice the subtle sensations of your breath coming in and out of your nose or with the rise and fall of your belly. You can practice breath awareness while sitting, walking, or listening to music. Once you feel comfortable, practice engaging your breath practice while dealing with difficult feelings or engaging in conversations with others. For instance, you can say to yourself something like, "I am breathing in peace. I am breathing out love."

IN PRACTICE

Take several deep breaths. What are you aware of now? Use these lines to write about what your senses capture.

_____

_____

_____

_____

_____

_____

HALF-SMILE

Engaging a half-smile is a valuable way to change your mental state and culti-vate a serene feeling in the moment. This practice involves relaxing your face and then slightly turning up your lips. As you smile, imagine your jaw softening and a relaxed feeling spreading across your face, your entire head, and down your shoulders. Start by practicing the half-smile while you feel calm, and eventually engage the practice while reflecting on a difficult event.

IN PRACTICE

What did you notice during the half-smile practice? In what ways can you imagine this practice being helpful in your life?

_____

_____

_____

_____

_____

BODY ACCEPTANCE

The body scan practice in chapter 2 offers another way to develop radical self-acceptance. You can use that practice, this time with the intention of accepting every sensation in your body. Bring acceptance and love to each part of your body: your feet, your legs, your pelvis, your belly, your back, your chest, your arms, your hands, your shoulders, your throat, and your head. You can place your hands over each part of your body, imagining rays of love permeating your body. Sometimes feeling the body can stir up uncomfortable sensations, emotions, or memories. Explore the concept of loving and accepting the pain. However, if this practice ever becomes too difficult, know that you can also pace yourself by sensing a body part and then bringing your awareness back out to your external environment.

IN PRACTICE

Explore the body acceptance practice. What are you aware of now? Did this practice bring up any painful feelings? Were you able to connect to any positive emotions? Use these lines to write about your experience.

_____

_____

_____

_____

POSITIVE SELF-STATEMENTS

The ultimate goal of all acceptance practices is to develop deep appreciation for yourself just as you are. Try saying, "I love myself just as I am in this moment." You can get more specific with this statement. For example, extend this acceptance toward your defenses. You can say, "I love myself even though . . . I push people away, I hurt myself sometimes, I yelled at my child." You can practice extending acceptance to your vulnerable emotions by saying, "I love myself even when I am . . . sad, afraid, embarrassed, ashamed."

IN PRACTICE

Explore what happens for you as you practice and personalize the positive self-statements. What are you aware of now? Did the practice bring up any emotions for you? Use these lines to write about your experience.

_____

_____

_____

_____

_____

_____

Choosing Change

Renee was ambivalent about letting go of her avoidance defenses, but she also recognized that it was time to learn a new way to be in the world. There was a part of her that believed she couldn't handle the stress, that there was something wrong with her. But there was also a new voice emerging. It emphatically said, "I know I can handle this, I am strong!" In our work together, I invited Renee to express and give words to each part of herself. She acknowledged the part that believed withdrawing helped her stay safe. She then gave voice to the part that recognized her need to let down her protective walls in order to really be happy. Renee said she felt stuck between these two sides of herself and she really wanted to be free.

It is common to feel ambivalent about change. You might find yourself bracing against change. You may feel afraid of becoming too vulnerable, groundless, or out of control. Releasing old patterns, addictive habits, or outgrown beliefs can feel destabilizing. Letting go can feel like a crisis. Surrendering to change takes courage. The following practices will help you explore your relationship to change:

HONORING AMBIVALENCE

Dr. Fritz Perls, founder of Gestalt psychotherapy, identified a common polarity between the part of self that is seeking growth and the part that is seeking safety. You may notice a part of you wants to let go of the patterns that no longer serve you, while another part is fearful and resistant to change. Attend to the voices representing each side of yourself. Treat each reason like an honored guest in your home, with an important voice that needs to be heard. When you ignore your fears, they are more likely to lead to self-sabotage. Consider if you have a tendency to dismiss any part of you as unimportant. Ultimately, resolution requires that you listen to, honor, and take responsibility for both sides of the polarity as it exists in you.

IN PRACTICE

In what ways do your habits or defenses help protect you? In what ways do they keep you safe? Write down all of the reasons you can think of about why you should stay the same and not change.

_____

_____

_____

_____

_____

In what ways are you ready to let go of old habits of self-protection? In what ways do the old habits interfere with your life or happiness? Write down all of the reasons you can think of for why you should change.

_____

_____

_____

_____

_____

FINDING EQUANIMITY AMIDST CHANGE

The term *equanimity* comes from the Buddhist insight meditation tradition. It is defined as the ability to stand in the middle of intensity, to develop patience with uncomfortable experiences, and to see the big picture as a way to maintain balance. Equanimity is sometimes inaccurately thought of as an attitude of distance and detachment. In actuality, you build equanimity by learning how to be in the discomfort of embarrassment, shame, discouragement, frustration, anger, and grief.

Ultimately, in order to change, you must step outside of your comfort zone and take a risk. Maybe this means going to the gym even though you feel out of shape and uncomfortable. Or perhaps this means journaling instead of eating when you are feeling sad. You might go to a long-avoided doctor's appointment despite your fears about your health. Your challenge might be to show your vulnerable emotions to a loved one instead of hiding your true feelings. In what ways do you need to step out of avoidance and face your fears?

> Remember to bring an attitude of curiosity to the In Practice exercises. Know that there are no right or wrong answers to the questions. If you become aware of painful emotions or memories, you can journal about them or bring in your experiences to discuss with your psychotherapist.

Going into the intensity of big emotions requires a groudwork of support and safety. What gives you the courage to step into your emotions, to feel yourself as chaotic, raw, fearful, or sad?

IN PRACTICE

This mindfulness practice is aimed to build your capacity to maintain a steady mind when stepping outside of your comfort zone.

Sit comfortably, and focus your awareness on your breath as it flows gently in and out. Place your hand over your heart, feeling the warmth of the touch of your hand on your heart. Focus on a sense of safety and ease. Gently breathe care and kindness into your heart. Notice the feelings and sensations that arise. Begin to reflect upon any changes that you would like to embrace in your life. Return your attention to the sensation of your hand over your heart. Breathe in and out as you say to yourself, "I trust in my capacity to handle change." Once again, reflect on any changes you would like to make. Get specific in your mind about what these changes look like for you. Return your attention to the sensation of your hand upon your heart. Once again, notice your breath as it flows gently in and out. Again say, "I trust in my capacity to handle change." Repeat this process for as long as it feels right for you.

Take a few minutes to write down anything that you are aware of now.

_____

_____

_____

_____

_____

DEVELOPING POSITIVE HABITS

Letting go of old, outgrown patterns requires identifying new, health-promoting behaviors. Imagine any new positive habits you could bring into your life. For example, if you are trying to stop sleeping during the day, you will best succeed if you're prepared with a range of positive actions you can take whenever you have an urge to lay down on the couch. You may choose to drink a glass of water, step outside for a brief brisk walk, or call a friend.

Letting go of unhealthy patterns requires that you develop new healthy habits. What new positive behaviors could you imagine creating space for in your life?

_____

_____

_____

_____

_____

Preparing for Trauma Work

Renee felt increasingly ready to address her painful past. She was learning to replace unhealthy survival strategies with positive coping strategies. Now when she felt the urge to avoid, pour a drink, or push her husband away, she practiced relying upon healthy and positive resources such as grounding, asking for help, and journaling.

All avoidance strategies disconnect or dissociate you from painful emotions and memories. Dr. Shapiro's EMDR therapy includes a preparation phase in treatment that focuses on helping you develop resources that will allow you to successfully process traumatic memories. When you feel safe and supported, you will be more capable of turning toward your difficult past. You will also strengthen your capacity to successfully handle current triggering relationships and events.

Resources are the tools that allow you to feel safe in the present moment. You can cultivate both internal and external resources to draw upon when you feel triggered into a trauma reaction. Resources can help restore a sense of inner calm and provide choices about how to respond to your environment. Internal resources include self-care practices that you have access to inside of your mind and body, such as deep breathing, grounding, containment, visualization, acceptance practices, mindfulness, exercise, and journaling. External resources are the tools that you call upon from your community and environment. These come in the form of reaching out to your therapist, talking to friends you can trust, spending time in nature, and creating a calm and predictable living space. While you will find a wide range of internal and external resources throughout this workbook, the following resources are particularly valuable in the early treatment phases of complex PTSD.

CREATING A HEALING SPACE

In the previous chapter (see page 50), you learned to develop an imagined safe place. To build on that, you can enhance your capacity to feel safe by developing an outer, real environment that reflects a peaceful and calm feeling. It can be difficult to find inner peace when the actual space around you is cluttered and chaotic. Choose a space in your living environment that you can claim as your healing space. Start by selecting a room, or even a corner of a room, within your home. Ideally this space is quiet and peaceful, and offers enough privacy for you to be vulnerable. If needed, create boundaries around your space by placing a screen or hanging a curtain. Think about what helps you hold your intentions of peace, ease, and safety. Perhaps you select some well-chosen quotes, images, or a candle. Maybe you want to have something from nature, such as flowers, a plant, or a stone. Explore colors or fragrances that soothe your senses. Try to keep your space free of clutter so that your peaceful space offers respite from the busyness of the outside world.

> "People are just as wonderful as sunsets if you let them be. When I look at a sunset I don't find myself saying, 'Soften the orange a bit on the right-hand corner.' I don't try to control a sunset. I watch with awe as it unfolds."
>
> —DR. CARL ROGERS, psychologist and author

IN PRACTICE

Set up a healing space in your home. You can use these lines to help you develop a plan for where you might create your space, and what you might bring into your space that helps convey a sense of peace and safety conducive to healing.

_____

_____

_____

_____

_____

GROUNDING

Grounding refers to using your ability to sense your body and feel your feet on the earth in order to calm your nervous system. Grounding is a key resource for trauma and emotional overwhelm. Your senses (hearing, seeing, smelling, tasting, touching) are the only necessary tools for anchoring yourself in the present moment. One simple practice involves naming five things you see, four things you hear, three things you can touch, two things you can smell, and taking one deep slow breath. You can mindfully increase your awareness by enhancing your sensory experience. For example, slowly eat a slice of a tart apple or choose an essential oil with a scent that you enjoy.

Grounding invites you to sense your body, notice your tension patterns, and surrender the weight of your physical body into gravity to feel the support of the earth. You can explore this practice while lying down on the ground. Release your weight into the points of contact with the floor beneath you. Notice how it feels to relax. Explore whether you feel safe. Make space for any emotions that arise in the process. You can evolve your practice of grounding by surrendering your weight to gravity while standing, and eventually while walking, slowly and mindfully. Keep your knees soft and not locked. When you walk, feel your feet rise and fall with each step. Can you stay connected to your emotions and sensations while moving? If you feel disconnected, slow down and come back to yourself in stillness.

IN PRACTICE

Explore the grounding practices. What do you notice in your body and mind? Did this practice bring up any uncomfortable feelings? Were you able to connect to any positive emotions? There is no right or wrong answer. Use these lines to write about your experience.

_____

_____

_____

_____

_____

_____

_____

_____

_____

_____

_____

_____

CONTAINMENT

As you get closer to addressing your trauma memories, you might struggle with emotions that feel too big or overwhelming. It's okay to step back and collect yourself. Healing trauma involves reclaiming a sense of choice about how, when, and where you feel your emotions. For example, you do not want to process traumatic memories in the grocery store or when you are parenting your children. You want to have safe and predictable places and ways to feel and process through difficult life events.

Sometimes you need to consciously compartmentalize difficult and distressing feelings, images, and thoughts in order to be present and to attend to your life activities. This is different than avoidance. Avoidance defenses involve an unconscious pushing away of distress. On the other hand, conscious containment practices can help you create distance from intense emotions with an agreement that you will also choose times to turn toward, address, and express the pain of trauma.

Another invaluable resource for trauma recovery is to develop an imagined container, a place that holds your distress. Some people use boxes. Others have file cabinets or wooden trunks. Your container can be a room in a house or a cave in nature with a rock that slides over the opening. It doesn't matter what kind of container it is, so long as it is big enough and strong enough to hold your painful thoughts, feelings, and memories when you are not actively engaged in processing your trauma. Some people even prefer to utilize a real container, such as a box or jar with a tight lid, to "put their problems into." Whether imagined or real, such a container can relieve you of negative thoughts.

> **Conscious containment practices can help you create distance from intense emotions with an agreement that you will also choose times to turn toward, address, and express the pain of trauma.**

Bring to mind an image of something that would be able to contain any and all of your difficult memories and feelings. When you have one in mind, take a good look at it. Note how this container opens and closes. When you close this container, it will remain tightly sealed until you choose to open it. Your container can only be opened by you. You can place a lock on your imagined (or real) container if you wish.

When you feel ready, think of something to place in your container for practice. This can be a worry, a difficult thought, or a recent disturbing event. Now, open your container, place your thought, feeling, or event into the container. Once it is inside, imagine your sealed and secure container, and the distance you have created from your worry.

Develop your own containment practice. Notice how you feel in your body, having set aside the distressing feeling. Notice any sensations of relief you may feel in your body: maybe your neck tension released or your shoulders have dropped. Notice your breath and the quality of your thoughts.

Use these lines to write about your experience.

_____

_____

_____

_____

Healing Allies

Sometimes it is hard to feel self-acceptance. Instead, you might feel highly critical or rejecting toward yourself. Healing allies are people or beings, either real or fictional, that you associate with nurturance, protection, and wisdom. When you find it hard to feel compassionate toward yourself, you can visualize your allies as a loving and healing presence.

When you choose an ally, you can think about characters from movies and books, a spiritual presence, admirable historical figures, or even animals you associate with strength. For example, one client's ally was Aslan, the lion from C. S. Lewis's *The Lion, the Witch and the Wardrobe*. He imagined the lion as a powerful presence that would protect and guide him. Another client thought of a friend who is a generous and giving mother to her children. She could imagine her friend's smiling and kind eyes gazing at her lovingly.

When thinking of an ally, choose someone with a caring and strong presence. What are character traits you associate with your ally? Perhaps you seek a feeling of warmth, a soft voice, or a fearless capacity to stand up to bullies. Can you imagine this character's strong, caring presence? Could you imagine them extending care to someone who is hurting or in pain? When you establish a high-quality ally, you would say, "Of course! This person would never reject anyone who is in pain; they would extend their strength to anyone who is hurting." Now, can you imagine this person extending care to you?

Notice how you feel while imagining your ally being there for you. Does your ally "have your back," offer wisdom, or provide loving care? Sometimes trying to find an ally can be challenging or can take time. Sometimes the inner critic steps in and says, "Who could ever love me? I'm not worth protecting!" If this happens to you, take a step back and realize that you are projecting your feelings about yourself onto your ally. As with all of the practices in this workbook, be gentle with yourself, take your time, and set a goal to remain curious about your experience.

IN PRACTICE

Explore developing a personal ally for yourself. If you were able to create a strong positive ally, reflect on how your body, mind, and breath responded. On the other hand, if you struggled with this practice, there is just as much value in writing about what happened for you. Use these lines to process your experience.

_____

_____

_____

_____

Turning Toward the Pain

Renee declared that she felt ready to deal with her painful history. She had already identified her childhood memories of wanting to run away when her mother was abusive. We began to look more closely at the feelings and beliefs associated with these difficult memories. Renee shared that she felt bad inside. Like she had done something wrong, but could never figure out *what it was. I asked her to sense her body. She said she felt tight across her belly, chest, and throat. She felt like she couldn't breathe.*

Then Renee recalled the time she stood in the doorway to her mother's room. She was around six years old and wanted a kiss goodnight. "I just wanted my mommy to come tuck me into my bed." But instead, her mother looked at her with disgust and screamed, "What is wrong with you, Renee?"

Renee began to cry. She said these were the very same words she found herself shouting to her kids.

She paused and looked at me and then said, "Deep down I have always believed that there was something wrong with me. I don't want my children to feel that way. They are beautiful; they are just being kids. They need me and that is healthy."

More importantly, Renee looked up with tears in her eyes and said, "What if there really isn't anything wrong with me either? I was just a kid too. I needed my mom to love me. The worst part is that she couldn't love me; not in the way that I needed. I see now that I am deserving of love, I do not need to push away the people who love me most."

Healing complex PTSD requires a willingness to change your relationship to pain. You may have invested a great deal of time and energy pushing your pain away or keeping a tight lid on your feelings. Ultimately, successful integration of childhood trauma involves processing and working through the beliefs, emotions, and body sensations associated with your painful memories. The resources you learned and practiced in this chapter are instrumental in preparing you for the deeper healing and hard work of trauma recovery. Chapters 4 and 5 will guide you into that process by teaching you restorative strategies to help you heal intrusive and depressive symptoms of C-PTSD. As you proceed to the following chapters that focus on healing intrusive and depressive symptoms of C-PTSD, continue to use the resources you've already learned here.

Chapter Takeaways

This chapter focused on identifying avoidance defenses, developing self-acceptance, acclimating to the fact that change is necessary, and developing resources for trauma recovery. Take the next several minutes to review the In Practice sections and any notes you have written down. What resonates with you now? Are there any resources for working with resistance that you found particularly helpful and would like to continue to practice? Remember, the goal of this phase of trauma treatment is to develop enough stabilization of symptoms so that you can begin to address traumatic memories without becoming overwhelmed or flooded. Do you feel that these resources have sufficiently prepared you for the work of healing trauma? If not, what else do you think you might need to feel that you are ready? Use this writing space as an opportunity to explore your answers to these questions.

4

Daniel's Story
Healing Invasive Symptoms

Daniel wasn't sure anyone was trustworthy. He'd had several doctors who never really understood him. One had diagnosed him with bipolar disorder; another with borderline personality disorder. He had been hospitalized twice because of self-harm and suicidal plans. He had been prescribed an assortment of medications, all of which left him feeling like he was living in a daze.

Then, Daniel began working with a psychiatrist who looked beyond his symptoms and diagnoses. This was the first doctor to express an interest in understanding the cause of Daniel's distress. He listened to Daniel's frustrations and came to understand that developmental trauma was the root of his symptoms. The doctor changed Daniel's diagnosis to PTSD and slowly tapered his medications. That doctor referred Daniel to my psychotherapy office for the treatment of complex PTSD.

When Daniel first entered my office, I could see that he had cuts up and down his arms. He could barely look me in the eyes. In time, he shared that he had a long and painful history of hurting himself in this way. He alluded to memories that invaded his life like unwelcomed guests and his reticence to leave his house because he never knew when he would get another flashback. He wasn't sure life was worth living and most definitely didn't want to live like this anymore. Together we began to unpack the burdens of Daniel's trauma history.

Daniel's story illustrates the intense distress that comes with invasive and intrusive symptoms of complex PTSD. Symptoms such as anxiety, panic, flashbacks, nightmares, hypervigilance, and emotional dysregulation can profoundly interfere with your ability to live the life you want. Through a multifaceted approach, this chapter will provide tools to challenge the thinking misconceptions associated with anxiety, and the skills that build healthy relationships. You will learn about the "window of tolerance" as it relates to emotion regulation. The primary goal of this phase of trauma treatment is to explore and process your personal history with compassion. Remember to pace yourself and to support yourself by practicing resources of self-acceptance, grounding, breath awareness, safe place imagery, and containment.

"Most people do not listen with the intent to understand; they listen with the intent to reply."
—STEPHEN R. COVEY, author and educator

Mind over Matter

"There were a few good years," said Daniel. Then he shyly admitted, "I went to college on a scholarship. I guess I'm pretty smart."

I learned that Daniel met a woman in college and they married after graduation. But a few years into his marriage, things began to fall apart. He left the marriage because he felt as though he was unraveling. When the doctors told him he had bipolar disorder or borderline personality disorder, he assumed they must be correct. He began to restrict the sphere of his life. He left his job, believing that he was too sick to work. He no longer went out socially. He was sure that people could tell there was something wrong with him. He needed to find a way out of the maze of his mind.

As humans, our thoughts profoundly influence our perceptions of ourselves and the world. This is not a new idea. Perhaps you were first introduced to the power of positive thinking by *The Little Engine that Could*. Against all odds, this small engine huffed and puffed his way up to the top of the mountain repeating, "I think I can, I think I can." We cannot always predict success; however, the likelihood of a positive outcome greatly increases when we change our thinking from "I can't" to "I can try."

Well-researched psychotherapy interventions from the field of cognitive behavioral therapy (CBT) emphasize challenging negative thoughts and changing them into more helpful and supportive ones. Typically, this technique involves keeping track of your thoughts in a journal so you can identify your thought patterns and their related emotions and behaviors. For example, if you tell yourself, "I know tomorrow's big meeting with my boss is going to be terrible!" you will likely feel anxious. As a result, you might have difficulties looking your boss in the eyes or speaking with confidence. However, if you said, "I can

> "... There is nothing either good or bad, but thinking makes it so."
> —WILLIAM SHAKESPEARE's *Hamlet*

handle presenting my ideas to my boss even if I am nervous," you might be able to prepare yourself with grounding and deep breathing prior to the meeting, leading to a more positive outcome.

It is important to note that you are not casting judgment on your thoughts as "good" or "bad." Rather, you are taking time to recognize that some thoughts are useful and others are less useful. Mindful awareness of body sensations as they relate to thoughts helps you to see that some thoughts create greater ease, whereas others create more distress.

Once you are aware of your negative or irrational beliefs, you can begin to replace them with more beneficial thoughts. For example, when you say to yourself, "This will never work," "What's wrong with me," or "I'm worthless," you reinforce self-limiting beliefs and painful emotions. Replacing these kinds of statements with more positive or useful ones—such as, "It's okay to be nervous," "Remember to breathe," or "Most people will accept me if I make mistakes"—will likely create a greater sense of possibility and positivity.

CHALLENGING THINKING ERRORS

Take a look at some of the common thinking errors that can amplify anxiety and interfere with your life:

- **All-or-nothing thinking:** This error is also called black-and-white or polarized thinking, and involves a tendency to view situations in only two categories rather than on a continuum. For example: "I always mess up, what is the point of trying?"
- **Catastrophizing:** This error involves believing that the very worst thing is going to happen without considering other more likely and less negative possibilities. Like a fortune-teller, you might try and predict the future, but with negative expectations. For example: "I just *know* that I will fail the test!"

- **Discounting the positive:** This error disqualifies or excludes positive experiences and qualities as if they do not count. For example: "She said I did well in the audition, but I bet she didn't mean it."
- **Emotional reasoning:** This error entails believing something is true because you feel it so strongly, while ignoring lacking or contrary evidence. For example: "I have an awful feeling about the party tonight; I'm sure I'll make a fool of myself."
- **Overgeneralization:** This error involves using current situations to develop broad conclusions about unrelated life experiences or events. For example: "Things never go my way; I have the worst luck."
- **Mind reading:** This error involves believing you know what others are thinking without considering other possibilities, and failing to check in with other people about what they are actually thinking. For example: "My friends think I'm stupid, I'm sure of it!"
- **Imperatives:** This error involves holding unrealistic and fixed standards such as "shoulds" toward yourself or others. In this case, you are critical when such standards are not met. For example: "I should have been able to speak up at the meeting; I'm such a wimp!"

CBT utilizes the act of disputing questions to challenge these thinking errors. Examples can include:

- Do I know for certain that the worst will happen?
- What evidence do I have that what I believe is actually true?
- Am I really able to predict the future?
- Is there another possible explanation for that person's behavior that isn't about me?
- Can I inquire about what that person is thinking/their reasoning?
- How can I accept, deal with, or cope with things being . . . (messy, imperfect, uncomfortable, etc.)?

IN PRACTICE

Take a few minutes to look over this list of thinking errors and write down any ones that you can relate to. See if you can identify specific examples of unhelpful thoughts that burden you in some way. Develop disputing questions to challenge your thinking errors.

_____

_____

_____

_____

_____

_____

_____

MANAGING MIXED MESSAGES

We learn messages about emotions early in life from our parents and caregivers. Some families are very emotionally expressive, while others are more subdued or even suppressed. Certain emotions might be treated differently than others, depending on the household. It is common to received mixed messages about emotions, which can lead to confusion. Here are some examples:

- "When I felt angry, my father got angrier. As a result, I became quiet and submissive. Anger feels scary and bad."
- "When I felt sad, my mother worried. Now I feel anxious instead of simply feeling sad."
- "It wasn't okay for me to be excited or happy. My parents always told me, 'Keep it down!' Now, I have learned not to care about life too much."
- "Whenever I was upset, my mom fed me. Now I can't tell if I'm feeling hungry or angry."
- "Nobody paid much attention to my emotions growing up. I was left to deal with my fears on my own. I still feel panicky and overwhelmed sometimes. I'm just 'too much' for anyone to handle."

- "I never knew what was coming my way. I have learned to keep a keen eye out for how others are feeling. This is how I protect myself."

Reclaiming a healthy relationship with your emotions entails reflecting upon the earliest education you had about feelings, challenging inaccurate messages, and developing new perspectives. Angry feelings, for example, are often a sign that someone has treated you poorly or that something is wrong. Rather than think that you must express or suppress your anger, see if you can harness the energy of anger to become more assertive, to clarify your boundary, or to become passionate about a needed change in your life.

If emotions were dismissed, disregarded, or misunderstood in your childhood home, it can be difficult to recognize how you feel now as an adult. You can, however, practice sensing your body to develop attunement to your feelings. Here are some body signals of the core emotions and positive messages about these feelings that you can incorporate into your life:

- **Sadness:** Feeling heaviness in your chest or a lump in your throat. Try saying to yourself, "Sadness needs to be felt and is a sign that I need care and compassion."
- **Anger:** Gritting your teeth and clenching your fists. You can say, "Anger offers valuable information and teaches me that I am worthy of fairness and kindness. I can assert my needs in healthy ways."
- **Fear:** Feeling shaky, breathless, or cold. Try saying, "Now, when I feel afraid, I can do something about it, then look around me and determine if I am safe now."
- **Shame:** Feeling a pit in your stomach and wanting to cover your face. Try saying, "My shame is a remnant of unwarranted feelings of unworthiness. I am worthy of love."
- **Disgust:** Feeling your lips curl downward while scrunching up your nose and a sour feeling in your stomach. Experiment with saying, "Feelings of disgust are signals that something isn't safe. I have a right to say no if it doesn't feel right."
- **Joy and excitement:** Feeling bouncy, energetic, smiling, and having a "glow" inside and on your face. Try saying, "I am allowed to be happy and free. I do not need to repress my joy."

Try to bring an attitude of curiosity and openness to exploration of your emotions. This will help you broaden your sense of self as you reclaim your emotional health.

IN PRACTICE

Take a few minutes to reflect on how emotions were handled within your family of origin. What messages did you receive about anger, sadness, fear, shame, or excitement and joy? Do you ever find it challenging to put your finger on how you are feeling? Does increasing your body awareness help? What messages would you like to tell yourself about your emotions now?

_____

_____

_____

_____

_____

_____

_____

_____

Interpersonal Effectiveness

Daniel began to share more about his marriage and the reason for his divorce. "We had a few good years, but then she wanted to have children," he said. "I started to have these horrible thoughts about hurting my wife. I couldn't bear to talk about them, and I felt I was living a dual life." Daniel felt haunted. He was fearful of the images in his head. He decided it was better if he wasn't around.

One of the most common reasons that clients come into psychotherapy is the pain associated with relationship stress and conflict. Interpersonal difficulties or losses can leave you feeling vulnerable and destabilized. A core dilemma of C-PTSD is that your longing for a relationship is in direct opposition to memories that tell you relationships aren't safe. As a result, developing healthy relationships can be challenging.

Importantly, living in the midst of ongoing relationship strife interferes with healing. Relationship crises can reenact painful relationship patterns that you learned in childhood. You can feel re-victimized or at risk of victimizing others. It is imperative that you feel safe at home in order to open the doors to your wounds from the past.

In even the healthiest of relationships, there will be moments of disconnection or unintentional misunderstanding. DBT skills that support interpersonal effectiveness will help you learn how to have healthy boundaries and resolve conflicts. Sometimes, this process involves admitting when you have caused harm and taking responsibility for your actions. At other times, you might need to refrain from taking responsibility for another person's harmful behaviors.

BOUNDARIES

Having a boundary is an aspect of self-respect that allows you to assert your "no" and your "yes." Without a boundary, you will be more likely to give in to others because you long for approval. Maintaining successful boundaries involves accepting the fact that you cannot please others all of the time. Boundaries are also meant to be flexible enough to allow for intimate connections with others. Ultimately, healthy boundaries require that you tolerate both closeness and separateness. Let's take a look at the three most common ineffective boundary patterns:

- **Unbounded:** If you have an unbounded boundary style, you may be hesitant to set clear limits with others for fear of rejection. You may tend to merge with others and in doing so, lose a sense of yourself for the sake of a relationship. You might be prone to taking care of others in lieu of yourself. If your boundaries are undefined, you might be prone to overriding your true feelings, which can result in resentment and anger. Healing involves a commitment to self-care and identification of your limits. Watch for a tendency to say yes without thinking things through.

- **Rigid:** If you have a rigid boundary style, you may have a tendency to withdraw from relationships. You might feel safest when you're self-reliant. Maybe you have constructed walls around your vulnerable feelings. When boundaries are too rigid, you can become isolated or carry a burdening belief that you always have to take care of things yourself. Healing involves allowing yourself to be vulnerable and recognizing that you have needs that others can and want to provide. Asking for what you need may feel uncomfortable at first, but doing so is a sign of growth and progress.
- **Combined:** The third and most common boundary style is actually a combination of the previous styles. You might alternate boundary styles between feeling a needy longing for connection and pushing people away when they get too close. Healing involves increasing your self-awareness about what boundary style is dominant at any given time. The need for closeness and space are both valid; however, you will feel greater satisfaction if you can advocate for those needs in healthy ways to your loved ones, such as speaking up when you need alone time to think, rather than pushing a loved one away. Healthy advocacy might involve saying, "I really need some alone time right now. I am going to go for a walk. I will be more available to connect with you when I get back."

Steps you can take to develop healthy boundaries include:

- **Self-awareness:** Mindfulness skills can help you develop awareness about what is motivating your behaviors. If you are acting out of fear of rejection or fear of intimacy, allow yourself to slow down and connect to your breath and your body.
- **Practice saying no:** An essential boundary skill is the ability to say no when something doesn't feel right to you. Absolving yourself of feelings of guilt and getting good at upholding your limits can take practice. Recognize that others may be disappointed with your choice, but this does not necessitate you giving in or getting angry.

- **Practice asking for what you need:** It is equally important to learn assertive ways to express your wants and needs. Practice asking for things and making requests. This process requires tolerating your own disappointment when requests are denied. Moreover, if your request is honored, you may need to challenge yourself to tolerate the closeness of someone taking care of you. Respectful self-advocacy for your needs is a way of acknowledging that you are worth being cared for.

IN PRACTICE

Look over the preceding common ineffective boundary patterns. Can you relate to any of these interpersonal relationship patterns? How so? Now look over the steps you can take to develop healthy limits. In what ways can you use these tips to strengthen the relationships in your life?

_____

_____

_____

_____

_____

_____

_____

_____

_____

_____

_____

CONFLICT RESOLUTION

Dialectical behavior therapy skills for interpersonal effectiveness include learning to address conflicts in an assertive yet caring manner. Effective communication skills involve "I statements" that do not blame or judge the other person. Healthy communication asks that you be aware of your own needs and have the ability to articulate them in an understandable way. In addition, healthy communication involves a desire to understand the other person's perspective and investment in a continued relationship. Conflicts happen in the best of relationships. Let's look at the strategies that facilitate successful conflict resolution:

- **Stay descriptive:** Describe your situation by naming the facts and avoiding judgmental statements. Notice a tendency to fall into the trap of statements that start with "You always . . . " or "You make me feel . . . " Here's an example of more effective descriptive language: "When I come home from work, I am aware that you want to talk with me about your day."
- **Name your feelings:** Talk about feelings, rather than assuming that the other person knows how you feel. For example, "I am tired when I come home, and it is hard to me to connect right away."
- **Ask for what you want:** Nobody can read minds. Express yourself by telling that person what you need. For example, "I would like to take 15 minutes after getting home to settle down after work. Then I can give you my full attention."
- **Ask what they need:** Asking the other person about their needs and wants shows that you care. It can be valuable to repeat back what you've heard to ensure that you understand them correctly. For example, "I hear that you want to connect with me at the end of the day. Is that correct?"
- **Give and take:** Healthy relationships generally involve some negotiation of both parties' needs. Let the other person know that you are willing to attend to their needs while continuing to advocate for your request. For example, "I will make sure that we have valuable and meaningful time together."
- **Back off as needed:** If you find yourself feeling rejected or defensive, it is important to take a few minutes and calm down. When taking a "time out," it is effective to make an agreement about how long you need and assert your commitment to resolve the conflict. For example, "I am starting to feel defensive. I am committed to you and to our conversation, but I need to catch my breath. Can we take a break and agree to come back in 10 minutes?"

Healthy interpersonal relationships are supported by communications that are clear, fair, and kind. Refrain from putting other people down and calling them names. Do your best to be respectful and truthful. If you have acted in a hurtful manner, being willing to admit it and apologize goes a long way to soothe hurt feelings.

IN PRACTICE

What are some of the relationship patterns and conflicts that occur in your life? Look over the strategies associated with successful conflict resolution. In what ways can you use these tools to strengthen the relationships in your life?

_____

_____

_____

_____

_____

_____

Emotion Regulation

Daniel spoke about how difficult it was to deal with his pain. There were times that he felt overwhelmed by uncomfortable feelings in his body. He would freeze or panic. For instance, he shared a recollection of the time a man looked at him "the wrong way" in the grocery store. Daniel left his cart with his groceries in the aisle, walked out of the store, and drove home in a daze. He remained numb for hours.

Emotion regulation is about reducing the suffering related to ineffective reactions to your emotions. The goal is not to get rid of your emotions; rather, feelings are simply meant to be felt. However, it is the painful accompanying feelings and actions—in Daniel's case, leaving the store and spending several hours in a daze—that you'll want to reduce, and can do so through emotion regulation. Like waves of the ocean, all emotions are meant to rise, crest, and retreat. Each day is different at the sea; the wind, currents, and tides are ever-changing. The first goal of emotion regulation is to sense the ebb and flow of your inner world so you may safely ride out even the biggest of storms. Let's talk about some of the issues that can cause the need for emotion regulation.

EMOTIONAL HIJACKING

Introduced by psychologist and author Dr. Daniel Goleman, the term *emotional hijacking* refers to the ways strong emotions such as fear or anger can overpower your thoughts and behaviors. There is a key structure within the limbic system of the brain called the amygdala, which functions like a smoke detector—it is wired to determine if you are in danger. If the answer is yes, your amygdala can temporarily inhibit your neocortex, the upper brain center responsible for rational and reflective thought. From an evolutionary perspective, it is better to immediately run from a tiger than to pause and think about it first.

Emotional hijacking initiates the instinctual fight-or-flight response. Unfortunately, individuals with a history of C-PTSD may be more prone to false alarms.

> Successful processing of traumatic memories allows you to say, "The traumatic event happened, it happened to me, and it is over now."

Intrusive symptoms such as flashbacks or extreme reactivity may be in reaction to perceived rather than actual threats. For instance, you might overreact to hearing your partner's annoyed tone of voice, getting interrupted during a conversation, or seeing your teenager roll their eyes when you ask them to clean their room. When you feel grounded and calm, these relatively minor events might have very little impact on you. However, when you feel more vulnerable, you're more likely to resort to impulsive behaviors.

Emotional hijacking is a common issue that benefits from the development of emotion regulation. You can buffer yourself from emotional hijacking by developing your emotional intelligence, or the ability to identify and respond effectively to emotions—both yours and those of the people around you. The goal is not to ignore your emotions; rather to harness the information that emotions provide as guidance for your life choices. If you find yourself emotionally hijacked, you can learn to intervene. Train yourself to interrupt the emotional flooding long enough to regain a sense of equanimity. Let's look at how:

- Try taking several slow, deep breaths to calm down your autonomic nervous system.
- Give yourself a timeout, and walk away from the triggering situation. Take some time to regroup and ground yourself.
- Observe your mind. Explore what you are telling yourself about the situation, and ask yourself if this is really true. Often there is a need to be right. Can you let go of the urge to prove anything for the time being?
- Create a short phrase you can say to yourself when you sense that you are losing your cool. You can try saying, "It's okay," "Calm down," or "Let it go."
- Increase your awareness of the emotional impact you have on others. Think of the image of a boat's wake on calm waters. What is the wake that you want to leave behind?

IN PRACTICE

Take a few minutes to review the previous section. Can you identify times that you have been emotionally hijacked? Look at some of the tools that can be used to slow down reactivity. Can you imagine implementing any of these into your life?

_____

_____

_____

_____

_____

_____

_____

WINDOW OF TOLERANCE

The *window of tolerance* is a concept developed by clinical psychiatrist Dr. Daniel Siegel. It refers to an optimal zone of nervous system arousal where you are able to respond effectively to your emotions. When you are outside of your window of tolerance, you will go into survival modes. Feeling anxious, overwhelmed, or panicked is a sign that you are hyper- or over-aroused, whereas feeling shut down, numb, or disconnected is a sign that you are hypo- or under-aroused. It is common with C-PTSD to alternate between the two extremes or to feel stuck in one or the other.

When you begin to practice emotion regulation, you focus on developing the capacity to stay within your window of tolerance by cultivating mindfulness of the fluctuations in your sensations, thoughts, and emotions. Through this, you increase awareness of the subtle signs of dysregulation. An early sign of distress might be a sense of slight irritability or growing frustration. Maybe you observe that your breath has become shallow or that you are clenching your jaw. When you are able to recognize the slight changes in your body, you can engage self-care resources before you get overwhelmed or shut down.

IN PRACTICE

What are the early signs of dysregulation that indicate you may be moving outside your window of tolerance? What are the self-care resources that worked for you in chapter 3? In what way can you imagine using these emotion regulation strategies before your situation becomes a crisis? Use these lines to write about your experience.

_____

_____

_____

_____

_____

_____

DISTRESS TOLERANCE

If the first goal of emotion regulation is to learn to sense the ebb and flow of your inner world, the second goal would be to increase the range of your window of tolerance. Having a trauma history tends to result in a reduced capacity for sensation and emotion. It is important learn how to exist with difficult feelings. You can do this by slowly developing your ability to stay present with increasingly greater amounts of sensation.

You can broaden your capacity to handle distress by slowly stepping out of your comfort zone. In somatic psychotherapy, you can learn to increase your window of tolerance through an activity called *pendulation*. Pendulation involves alternating your attention between feelings of safety and feelings of distress as they are experienced in your body. The practice goes as follows:

- Within a safe environment, choose a recent distressing event to think about. Depending upon your comfort level, you can choose a relatively minor recent event or perhaps one where you found yourself triggered outside your window of tolerance. Mindfully observe any emotions, thoughts, and body sensations that you experience as you recall the event. Bring your attention to the areas of your body where you feel tension or discomfort. Stay with the sensations for a few breaths.
- Choose a descriptive word for your distress. Your word can correspond to a sensation, an emotion, a color, or an image. Some examples are "jumpy," "angry," "hot," "locked," "fear," or "dark."
- Now, bring your attention to any area of your body where you feel calm and at peace. Maybe this resides around your heart, or perhaps in your hands or your legs. If you are unable to find any positive sensation, look for an area of your body that feels neutral. Again, allow your awareness to reside here for a few breaths.
- Choose a descriptive word for your calm or neutral sensation. Again, your word can correspond to a sensation, an emotion, a color, or an image. Some examples are "relaxed," "peace," "free," "clear," "empty," or "light."
- Now begin to alternate your attention back and forth between the distressing and calm sensations. Think about your distressing event, feel your sensations,

and connect to your descriptive word. See if you can stay with the uncomfortable experience just a little longer. Then, return your attention to your calm or neutral sensation, any related image, and descriptive word. Perform several rounds, alternating your attention between your calm place and the distressing event.

- Notice any new sensations in your body, including the desire to breathe deeply, let go with a sigh, or move your body in response to your felt experience. Perhaps you feel the impulse to shake or push your arms or legs. These impulses are part of sequencing—a normal and healthy resolution of the fight-or-flight reaction. Follow any urges to move until you feel complete.

Once you feel familiar with your pendulation practice, you can choose to try it with a distressing trauma memory from your past. However, if this is new for you, it is wise to instead unwind traumatic material with a somatic psychotherapist who is familiar with Peter Levine's Somatic Experiencing® therapy.

IN PRACTICE

Take some time to write about your experience of your pendulation practice. What were the descriptive words you chose? Where did you feel distress in your body? Where did you find a calm or neutral sensation? What did you notice as you alternated your attention between your distressing and calm or neutral sensations? Use these lines to write about your experience.

_____

_____

_____

_____

_____

_____

_____

_____

_____

_____

YOGA ON THE EDGE

Yoga offers an opportunity to reframe your relationship to discomfort as an awakening of the heart. This activity brings present, centered attention to the body, breath, and mind. The aim is to meet your "edge" of sensation by holding postures just long enough so that your mind is compelled to pay attention. If you hold too far back from the edge, you will have too little sensation to work with and the practice will remain superficial. Signs that you are going over your edge are the loss of connection to your breath or a sensation of sharp pain. Pay attention to these signals to avoid hurting yourself.

In yoga, you'll learn to listen carefully to the wisdom of your body. As you deepen into postures, you might notice that fear arises. You may want to run. You have a choice to either stay with your experience or back away. You might feel irritable or uncomfortable. Often, staying with the sensations of your edge can create powerful internal change. You might experience a surge of emotion or a desire to move your body to release a buildup of sensations. The aim is to surrender to this experience.

My training in Kripalu yoga emphasized that *will* and *surrender* are polarities that need to exist in balance. Like two wings of a bird, they need to function in tandem to create flight. Too much force and you risk becoming rigid and hard. Too much emphasis on surrender and you risk becoming stagnant or overflexible. Yoga postures that are part of a willful practice include warrior poses, heart openers, and balancing postures. Yoga postures that emphasize surrender include child's pose, forward folds, and restful yogic relaxation practices.

When you pay attention to your body, you will get feedback about when to push yourself and when to soften. Is there a sharp pain? Are you holding your breath? These are signs to back off. Do you feel tired or uninterested? Does your posture feel dull? These are signs to deepen your practice and engage in a new challenge. The most important part of the practice is your commitment to listen honestly to your sensations and emotions.

Understanding Your History

Daniel and I began to explore his history in greater depth. Now armed with tools for distress tolerance, he was able to remain mindful of his emotional fluctuations while talking about the past. He shared that his father was an alcoholic who physically abused him and his brother. The worst part was when he had to stand there and watch his brother get hurt. He hated the feelings of helplessness. He described feeling disgust toward his mother, who stood by and did nothing to protect him. Little by little, he spoke about his awful past.

Daniel also spoke about a teacher in the sixth grade who saw his intelligence. Quietly, Daniel said, "She was the first person to believe in me."

He elaborated, "It was because of her that I survived. Later, she helped me to leave home. It was because of her that I got a scholarship to go to college."

In order to heal from C-PTSD, it is essential to turn toward your trauma history. Successful integration of traumatic memories involves processing parts of your painful past, bit by bit. If you feel overwhelmed, you can pace yourself by only addressing one memory or even part of a memory at a time; breaking down the healing process into small, accessible chunks. Acknowledging what happened to you is the first part of the healing process.

CULTIVATING COHERENCE

There is power in being able to tell your story. According to Dr. Bessel van der Kolk, a clinical psychiatrist recognized for his work in post-traumatic stress, healing from trauma involves putting unspeakable events into words. Likewise,

Dr. Daniel Siegel discusses the importance of "coherence" as a key component to healing from a traumatic childhood. Coherence is best defined as having a story that makes sense. This does not mean that you feel okay about what happened to you. Rather, coherence involves having an understanding about your past and how it informs who you are today. Let's look at what facilitates coherence:

- Mindful reflection on your life, including traumatic losses
- Awareness of how your unique life experiences have made you who you are
- Development of an inclusive narrative or life story that organizes your self-understanding, accommodates new information, and supports your ongoing growth

This next practice poses questions to help you explore your childhood history as a foundation for developing a coherent narrative. These questions ask you to reflect on the nature of your relationships with family members and caregivers, as well as events of abuse or neglect. This practice will help you identify traumatic events that remain triggers that cause you to feel destabilized in your current life. Some questions will also look for the presence of positive resilience factors in order to identify your potential resources or allies for healing.

Be mindful that you might experience uncomfortable feelings and emotions. If you find yourself landing on any hot spots of traumatic memories, give yourself permission to only write the overarching theme rather than the specifics of the events. Imagine that you are writing the headline of a newspaper article, rather than going into the details of the story. You can pace yourself and slow down the process by only answering one question at a time, or declining to answer any question that brings up too much discomfort. Remember that you can turn toward your resources such as grounding, safe place, or containment as needed. If you are working with a therapist, you can also discuss your answers to these questions within the safety of that relationship.

IN PRACTICE

What was the nature of your relationship with your mother when you were growing up?

_____

_____

_____

What was the nature of your relationship with your father when you were growing up?

_____

_____

_____

Were there any other parental figures (e.g. stepparents, grandparents, caregivers) that took care of you when you were a child? If so, describe those relationships.

_____

_____

_____

Did you have any siblings? If so, describe those relationships.

_____

_____

_____

How did your primary caregivers respond to you when you were upset (sad, angry, hurt, or afraid)?

_____

_____

_____

How did your parents discipline or not discipline you as a child?

_____

_____

_____

Do you know of early separations from your parents? Do you recall experiencing physical or emotional neglect?

_____

_____

_____

Do you recall experiences that were abusive (verbally, physically, or sexually)?

_____

_____

_____

What was the relationship like between your parents? Do you recall episodes of anger or violence? Did they get divorced?

_____

_____

_____

Were any of your caregivers living with an untreated mental illness? If yes, what impact did this have on you?

_____

_____

_____

Were any of your family members addicted to alcohol or drugs? If yes, how did this affect you?

_____

_____

_____

Did any of your family members spend time in jail or prison? If yes, what impact did this have on you?

_____

_____

_____

Were there any positive mentors who were invested in you, cared for you, under-stood you, or protected you during your childhood? Was there someone who noticed that you were capable, intelligent, or talented?

_____

_____

_____

Do you recall having a community member (such as a neighbor, church member, teacher, or coach) who was there to help you? Do you recall having someone who cared how you were doing at home or in school?

_____

_____

_____

Did you develop any friendships in which you could talk about your life and feel understood?

_____

_____

_____

Did you develop street smarts: were you independent, or a go-getter?

_____

_____

_____

Now, take a look at your answers to the previous questions. Can you identify traumatic events that might exist as triggers in your current life?

_____

_____

_____

TRANSGENERATIONAL TRAUMA

When developing an understanding of yourself and your trauma history, it can be valuable to broaden your perspective to include *transgenerational trauma*. Psychotherapists have long recognized that relational, behavioral, and emotional patterns can be traced across generations. Looking at your family tree can provide a deeper understanding of you as an individual. Transgenerational trauma refers to the ways that unresolved trauma of one generation becomes a legacy that is passed down to the next generation.

Research by traumatic stress expert Dr. Rachel Yehuda reveals that PTSD runs in families. Children of trauma survivors with PTSD are significantly more likely to develop PTSD when exposed to traumatic events. For instance, this pattern is seen in adult children and grandchildren of Holocaust, Hiroshima and Nagasaki survivors, and war refugees. Furthermore, Dr. Siegel suggests that adults who have unresolved childhood trauma can lack a coherent narrative about their past. When these adults become parents, they have a reduced capacity to be mindful about the way their emotions and actions impact their children. These parents are more likely to become hijacked by emotions of jealousy, resentment, or anger, leading to abusive or neglectful behaviors.

Psychotherapy focused on healing transgenerational trauma involves some detective work to understand your family history. Unpacking family legacies can be uncomfortable for family members who are invested in seeing that the past stays in the past. Trauma stories can function like sworn secrets that have been tightly tucked away or only referred to in whispered voices. In contrast, other parents can inadvertently overexpose children with frequent retellings or reenactments of traumas from the past.

As you gather information about your family's previous generations, try to look for significant life events and patterns. For example, you might notice patterns of alcoholism or strife between mothers and daughters that can be traced back for many years. Looking back at your transgenerational legacies, you might find gifts there as well; strengths such as perseverance, humility, and sacrifice that allow you to be alive today.

Your family history can provide insight into your own predispositions. Furthermore, research by Dr. Marshall Duke at Emory University suggests that attending to family stories enhances your emotional health. Research indicated that individuals who knew more about their family ancestry were better able to manage the effects of traumatic stress after 9/11 and Hurricane Katrina. More specifically, individuals with an internal narrative about the ups and downs of their family history showed the greatest resilience.

IN PRACTICE

Take the time to reflect on the influences and experiences from the generations that preceded you. What do you know about the childhood experiences of your parents? What were the hardships that they faced? How did they cope? What do you know about the life experiences and hardships faced by your grandparents? Do you know anything of your earlier generations? As you reflect on your family history, what patterns do you observe, positive or negative? Are you aware of any accomplishments and strengths within your family lineage?

Take some time to write out your answers to these questions.

_____

_____

_____

_____

_____

_____

_____

Processing the Past

Daniel talked about the painful memories of his past. He expressed his feeling of helplessness. He acknowledged the rage and disgust he felt toward both of his parents. As he processed his memories of these childhood horrors, Daniel described feeling that his body felt tight everywhere. He felt like he might explode. As he maintained awareness of his sensations, he had an impulse to imagine locking his father up and putting him where he belonged: behind bars. He then visualized saving his brother and the two of them escaping to freedom.

Then a deep sadness arose as Daniel said, "I have a feeling that my father was abused, too. I wish that he could have found freedom."

Daniel's anger at himself began to subside. He forgave himself for not being able to do anything to stop his father's cruel abuse. He acknowledged, "I was just a young boy; I did the best I could."

All trauma treatment therapies ask you to review traumatic events that happened to you. The goal is to desensitize yourself to the traumatic event. Desensitization is defined as a reduction in the amount of emotional and somatic distress that you feel when you think about a traumatic event. Importantly, this lessened intensity is not the same as avoiding or dissociating from your pain. Quite the contrary, you have faced it, and in doing so, you've tipped the scales to reduce its power over you. Successful processing of traumatic memories allows you to say, "The traumatic event happened, it happened to me, and it is over now."

DESENSITIZATION

Desensitization involves reflecting on a traumatic event with sensory details, thoughts, and feelings resulting in a reduction of the amount of emotional and somatic distress associated with the traumatic event. There are several approaches to desensitizing traumatic memories. Exposure therapy involves talking about the traumatic events repeatedly until you feel the intensity decrease. However, this model can lead you to feel overwhelmed or re-traumatized. More nuanced models of desensitization include cognitive processing therapy (CPT) and eye movement desensitization and reprocessing (EMDR) therapy.

CPT emphasizes that successful processing of traumatic memories requires you to identify thoughts that interfere with trauma resolution. Together with your therapist, you can learn to recognize the presence of "stuck points," such as sweeping overgeneralizations like "I can never trust anyone" or inaccurate logic such as "If only I had done X, then I could have prevented Y from happening." CPT involves a very specific set of instructions for clients to write about a traumatic incident with as many sensory details (sights, sounds, smells, etc.) as possible. With the support of your therapist, you should try to include any thoughts and feelings that you remember occurring during the event. You are encouraged to read your written account to yourself daily and then to read your narrative to your therapist at your next session. However, please remember that you can pace yourself by skipping any In Practice sections that feel overwhelming, returning to your resources as needed.

> "Where there had been only fearful emptiness or equally frightening grandiose fantasies, an unexpected wealth of vitality is now discovered. This is not a homecoming, since this home has never before existed. It is the creation of home."
> —DR. ALICE MILLER, psychologist and author

EMDR therapy emphasizes that desensitization is the result of your innate capacity to adapt to adversity and process difficult life events. Desensitization requires that you enter a dual awareness state (DAS). You can think of this as having one foot in the present moment and one foot in the past trauma memory. If you step both feet into the feelings, sensations, and images of your traumatic past, you are more likely to become flooded or overwhelmed. DAS is achieved through the use of bilateral stimulation as you focus on an image associated with the trauma. Most commonly, bilateral stimulation is achieved by moving your eyes from side to side in short sets that are guided by your therapist. EMDR therapy does not require that you retell the trauma story. Rather, you visualize the trauma image with the bilateral stimulation, and track your present-moment somatic sensations, thoughts, and images. Sometimes you can feel stuck while working through traumatic memories. For example, you might be caught up in believing inaccurate beliefs such as "The abuse was my fault" or "I am bad." In this case, you and your EMDR therapist can work together to challenge negative thinking patterns that can interfere with trauma processing.

A wide body of research by Dr. James Pennebaker from the University of Texas indicated that simply writing about traumatic memories produces positive mental and physical health outcomes such as improved mood, better mental outlook, improved immune system functioning, and reduced blood pressure. You can write about traumatic events from the privacy of your home as a supplement to therapy, or as self-healing when psychotherapy is not accessible or affordable. The greatest benefit comes from writing about:

- The facts and details of the traumatic event
- Any thoughts, emotions, or sensations that you experienced during the event
- The feelings, beliefs, or images you have about the event now
- The impact that you believe this event had on your life

When writing about traumatic events, it is helpful to let go of your inner critic or any desire to keep your writing socially acceptable. Therapeutic writing encourages you to freely associate about the traumatic event and to be open to following your train of thought, wherever it takes you.

IN PRACTICE

Earlier in this chapter (see page 116), you were introduced to a series of questions about your family history. At that time, did you identify any traumatic events that would benefit from further attention? This exercise offers an opportunity to go into greater depth by processing a traumatic memory through the act of writing.

You can start by writing in the space provided here, or you may choose to write in a journal where you will have unlimited room. You can repeat this exercise as needed by writing about additional traumatic events.

_____

_____

_____

Integration

Daniel had an important realization. He understood that he had been punishing himself for not being able to protect his brother. After processing his traumatic memories, he was able to say, "I know now it wasn't my fault."

He was finally able to grieve for his childhood, for the loss of his marriage, and for the ways that he had hurt himself over the years. In time, his suicidal fantasies became a thing of the past. He was finally ready to live his life. He longed to come out of isolation, to reengage in the world and develop healthy relationships with others.

The previous In Practice section encouraged you to write about a traumatic event from your past. Perhaps you discovered new insights, increased your self-understanding, or developed a deepened sense of compassion. These positive emotions are a common outcome of processing trauma. It can take some time to incorporate this new awareness into your life. The next phase of trauma treatment focuses on integration of new insights into meaningful action and change. Chapter 5 guides you through several restorative practices for healing depressive symptoms of C-PTSD and provides tools for the integration of the insights you have gained in this workbook.

Perhaps you felt overwhelmed by the writing practice. If you felt flooded, overwhelmed, or outside of your window of tolerance, were you able to ground, contain, and return to a feeling of safety? If your answer is no, this is simply a sign to seek out more support. Healing from C-PTSD can bring up vulnerable emotions, and a workbook is not a replacement for the in-person support of a psychotherapist. Remember, if anything starts to feel too painful, you can always pace yourself by putting this book down or returning to the preparatory resources and acceptance practices in chapters 2 and 3. There is nothing wrong with slowing down the process if you need more time to integrate new information. Again, I strongly encourage you to seek out a qualified therapeutic professional, especially if you need more support than self-help can provide.

Chapter Takeaways

This chapter guided you to work with invasive and intrusive symptoms of complex PTSD. You explored common thinking errors associated with anxiety, developed tools to support healthy relationships, and learned about the window of tolerance as it relates to emotion regulation. Moreover, you had opportunities to deepen your self-understanding and process traumatic events of your past. Take the next several minutes to review the In Practice sections throughout this chapter and any notes you have written. What have you learned about yourself, your emotions, and your relationships? In what ways has your past influenced who you are today? Use this writing space as an opportunity to reflect on your experience thus far.

5

CHAPTER FIVE

Kathy's Story
Healing Depressive Symptoms

Kathy, a bright single woman in her mid-forties, came into my office having already been through several years of therapy elsewhere. She knew her story well, and was able to give a clear summary of her traumatic past. In our first session, I learned that Kathy had been sexually abused, starting at the age of six, by her father. The abuse had gone on for five years undetected. Her mother was "checked out." When Kathy was 11, she finally told her mother about the abuse, and the two of them left the state. She never saw her father again. She left her home, her friends, and her community. Kathy and her mother moved five more times throughout her childhood.

Though she's been in therapy for a while, Kathy remains burdened by pervasive feelings of hopelessness and despair. "I still feel so depressed and I am constantly exhausted," Kathy said to me through her tears.

I later learned that Kathy suffered from stomach problems and chronic back pain that caused her to miss work due to frequent doctor's appointments. "I'm worried that I will lose my job," she expressed. She felt plagued by feelings of embarrassment and shame. She asked, "What is wrong with me that I can't get better?"

> "It is one thing to process memories of trauma, but it is an entirely different matter to confront the inner void."
> —DR. BESSEL VAN DER KOLK, psychiatrist

Kathy's story describes the pervasive nature of depressive symptoms and the toll that trauma can take on the body and mind. Depressive symptoms of complex PTSD are often the hardest to resolve. Feelings of hopelessness, helplessness, despair, and shame can dominate your reality. When your mental and physical well-being becomes compromised, it is hard to see a way out.

If you can relate to Kathy's story, know that you are not alone. About 1 in 10 adult Americans have some type of depression; however, depression is nearly four times more likely if you have a history of trauma. Depression can cause you to lose interest in things you used to enjoy. Perhaps you sleep and eat more or less than you would like. Maybe you feel worn out or don't have the desire to do anything. You might believe things will never change, or wonder what's the point of trying.

It is important to recognize that the hopeless thoughts and feelings are part of the depression itself. These symptoms are remnants of your former existence in an environment where you were threatened and helpless to change the situation. Through a multifaceted approach, you will learn ways to compassionately work with any depressive symptoms. This chapter will help you unwind any unresolved feelings of shame and helplessness. The goal of this phase of trauma treatment is to support your physical and emotional wellness by integrating new positive feelings and beliefs about yourself into your life.

The Depression Trap

Kathy feared that she would always be depressed. Feeling defeated, Kathy said, "I have no hope that I will ever get better."

Kathy and I began to explore some of the beliefs that she had about herself and her symptoms. I learned that she internalized a core belief that she is permanently damaged. I asked what her life might be like if she let go of that belief. She reflected on the question for several minutes and finally replied, "I wouldn't know who I am."

Gently I replied, "Then who would you like to become?"

Most people with C-PTSD must confront the hopeless thoughts, painful emotions, and intolerable sensations of depressive symptoms. Cognitive behavioral therapy suggests that there is a triad of negative thinking associated with depression. This triad consists of a negative view of the self, a negative view of the world, and a negative view of the future. For instance, you might say, "I am a failure, bad things always happen to me, and nothing is ever going to change." These beliefs are derived from learned helplessness and shame. Dissociation is common when you feel helpless. Freeing yourself from the trap of depressive symptoms requires gentleness, acceptance, and persistence.

LEARNED HELPLESSNESS

When there is no way to stop an abuse, end a situation of domestic violence, or convince a parent to stop drinking, a child feels powerless. Persistent childhood trauma is characterized by a state called *learned helplessness*. This term was initially introduced to describe how animals that were repeatedly exposed to an unavoidable shock would make no attempt to escape, even when given an opportunity to exit. Psychologist and researcher from the University of Pennsylvania Dr. Martin Seligman later extended an understanding of learned helplessness to people who feel and behave in a helpless manner when they have no control over a threatening situation. He suggested that learned helplessness was the base of a pessimistic attitude. He identified the 3 P's of pessimism: Personalizing, Pervasiveness, and Permanence. In other words, it's like saying: "It's my fault, I mess everything up, and I will always be this way."

When you have been raised by untrustworthy caregivers, it is common to generalize your experience—you may feel as though no one can be trusted or that the world is completely dangerous. As you heal from C-PTSD, it's important to recognize that you are safe now and have choices now. You are no longer stuck in the powerlessness of your past. Dr. Seligman suggests adopting a positive set of thoughts he calls "learned optimism." This process is achieved by consciously challenging negative self-talk and replacing inaccurate thoughts with positive beliefs.

IN PRACTICE

Can you relate to the cognitive triad of depression and the 3 P's of pessimism? What core beliefs tend to hold you back? If you were to let go of these beliefs, what do you imagine your life might look like? What would you like to be able to tell yourself now?

_____

_____

_____

_____

_____

_____

_____

_____

_____

_____

_____

_____

HEALING SHAME

Shame is characterized by believing that you are "bad." This emotion is based upon a distorted sense of yourself as being unworthy, damaged, or a failure. Why is shame so pervasive? Young children are completely dependent upon caregivers for a sense of safety and connection in the world. As discussed earlier in the book, if you had an abusive caregiver, you faced a critical conflict: your biological drive to seek closeness from the very source of the terror you were trying to escape. Adults who were abused or neglected as children will often blame themselves. This can lead to persistent feelings of guilt and shame. EMDR therapist Dr. Jim Knipe proposes that this self-blame is a direct link to childhood logic—children will develop a fantasy that they are bad kids relying upon good parents to avoid confronting the terrifying reality that they are good kids relying upon bad parents.

"... We cannot eliminate the so-called negative forces of afflictive emotions. The only way to work with them is to encounter them directly, enter their world, and transform them. They then become manifestations of wisdom. Our weaknesses become our strengths, the source of our compassion for others, and the basis of our awakened nature."

—DR. JOAN HALIFAX,
Buddhist teacher and author

Shame is often hidden underneath perfectionism. As a child, you may have internalized the belief that you had to act perfect because your parents couldn't handle your authentic feelings. Or perhaps you believed acting "good" would stop the bad things from happening. In either situation, you may have had to hide your true feelings to avoid rocking the boat. Perfectionism is maintained by critical self-talk that attempts to push down painful feelings. When the inner critic berates you for being lazy, stupid, or useless, you are again confronted with your shame.

Let's take a closer look at some practices that can free you from the cycles of shame and perfectionism:

- **Explore your use of language:** Dr. Siegel points out the difference between saying "I am bad" and "I feel bad." The first statement reflects identification with a painful emotion, whereas the second statement allows for recognition of a feeling without being consumed by it.
- **Avoid "shoulds":** "Shoulds" are one way of pushing perfectionism or perceived expectations on yourself and rejecting your authentic presence. You might say, "I should be over this by now," "I shouldn't make mistakes," or "I should be strong." When you say or think the word "should," I invite you to step back and instead focus on self-acceptance.
- **Imagine shame is a bully:** Seeing shame as a bully can give you some space from the emotions and allow you to talk back! How do you feel when the shame bully puts you down? What do you want shame to know? If you have a hard time standing up to shame, you can bring in your ally from chapter 3 (see page 90) for reinforcements. Who would stand up for you and protect you? What would you and your ally say to the shame bully?
- **Experience the body's sensations of shame:** Often the most difficult part of healing shame is tolerating that felt sense in your body. Words can hardly describe the often intolerable "yuck" that accompanies shame. You might experience an encompassing sinking feeling or a vague sensation as though you did something wrong. A valuable practice for unwinding the somatic experience of shame is to return to the pendulation practice from chapter 4 (see page 111). The goal is to slowly build tolerance for the physical discomforts that accompany shame. Once you can feel your body, you have greater choice about how to move and breathe. There is tremendous power in reclaiming your body from shame. Perhaps you find a posture that feels strong and capable, or maybe you place your hands over your heart in a gesture of loving kindness.
- **Invite vulnerability:** When feeling shame, it is common to hide your true feelings for fear of further embarrassment. Showing people how you really feel allows them to support you. Dr. Brené Brown's research has shown that

expressing one's most vulnerable feelings is a sign of strength and facilitates health. She explains, "We cannot selectively numb emotions. When we numb the painful emotions, we also numb the positive emotions."

IN PRACTICE

How does shame show up in your life? What thoughts or sensations accompany shame for you? Explore the preceding practices when shame intrudes in your life. What helps you overcome or heal from shame?

_____

_____

_____

_____

_____

_____

_____

_____

_____

HEALING DISSOCIATION

Dissociation is a biological protection that disconnects you from threatening experiences. It exists on a continuum from relatively mild sensations of fogginess, sleepiness, or having difficulty concentrating to feeling numb or cut off. In the most extreme situations, you might have lapses of memory or a feeling of lost time. For instance, a neglected or abused child may learn to dissociate from, or tune out, threatening experiences. In adulthood, this dissociation can be perpetuated as you push away the parts of you that hold emotions of fear, shame, or helplessness. Here you might say, "It's just too much to know what happened."

Derealization and *depersonalization* are two key aspects of dissociation. Derealization refers to ways in which you feel surreal or as if you are living in a dream. Depersonalization is when you disconnect from your feelings or thoughts as though they are not yours.

Healing dissociation asks you to accommodate the reality of your childhood neglect or abuse. In doing so, you develop the capacity to recognize that traumatic events happened to you and that they are over now. You can differentiate the past from the present, which gives you access to choices now that were not available to you then. This process asks you to develop your understanding of injustice, unfairness, suffering, or evil as it exists in your life and the world—this plays a crucial role in your ability to adapt to adversity. Dr. Viktor Frankl's story of surviving his years as a prisoner in a Nazi concentration camp exemplifies this process. He observed that those prisoners who were able to retain a sense of meaning could maintain hope, and therefore were most likely to survive the atrocities.

> "The question we should be asking is not, why did this happen to me? What did I do to deserve this? That is really an unanswerable, pointless question. A better question would be, 'Now that this has happened to me, what am I going to do about it?'"
>
> —DR. HAROLD KUSHNER, rabbi and author

Meaning can be found in many ways. It can come in the form of philosophy, religion, or spirituality. Meaning can also come about through recognizing how your unique and painful life experiences have helped you grow or become a better person in some way. Importantly, nobody has a right to tell you that your traumatic life events happened for a reason. No matter what concepts resonate with you, the meanings you take must be of your own choosing and must feel right to you.

What are your thoughts and feelings after reading about dissociation? What gave you meaning before reading this book? Has any new meaning begun to surface? Describe your thoughts.

_____

_____

_____

_____

_____

_____

_____

Trauma and Grief

Kathy was no longer blaming herself for her depression. She felt a slight glimmer of hope. Nonetheless, she still felt the heaviness of her depression and continued to cry almost every day. We explored the underlying cause of her sadness by talking about the many losses she has faced in her life. She began to grieve—for the loss of her community, her friends, and her childhood home. She even grieved the loss of her father. Even though he was abusive, she was still sad that she never saw him before he died. She reflected, "I never even said goodbye."

Kathy had so many feelings about his death—anger, relief, sadness, redemption. She said it was confusing to have so many emotions about the same person.

Trauma often involves grief. You might grieve the loss of your safety. Maybe you grieve missed joys of childhood. Additionally, loss of those who were neglectful or abusive can bring forward unresolved pain and feelings of resentment. Grieving involves letting go. However, releasing traumatic memories can sometimes feel at first like you are letting go of any last remnants of hope for redemption.

Cognitive processing therapy (CPT) recognizes that unresolved grief can complicate recovery from PTSD and lead to depressive symptoms. Importantly, grief is not a disorder. It is a normal reaction to loss and does not have a timeline. CPT aims to remove the barriers that interfere with the natural course of grief. For example, distorted thoughts can block grief by either denying the reality of the loss or making you inaccurately blame yourself. You may have received messages that you need to "be strong," and therefore have learned to hide your pain. By developing more accurate beliefs about yourself and the world, you can foster a healthier relationship to grief and accept the reality of any losses you have faced.

STAGES OF GRIEF

Grief is complex and can be disorienting. Models of the grief process can help you find your bearings. Classically, psychiatrist and author Dr. Elisabeth Kübler-Ross identified five core stages of grief as denial, anger, bargaining, depression, and acceptance. More importantly, Dr. Kübler-Ross encouraged her readers to refer to these stages lightly—they are neither universal nor linear. Nonetheless, the stages of grief offer a way to validate and talk about feelings related to death and loss. Later models of grief recognize that resilience, hope, and growth are also essential components of the grieving process; that attending to loss will bring about feelings of gratitude and forgiveness.

> "There is nothing in the world, I venture to say, that would so effectively help one survive even the worst conditions, as the knowledge that there is a meaning in one's life."
> —DR. VIKTOR E. FRANKL,
> psychiatrist and Holocaust survivor

ness. Allow this review of the core aspects of grief to help you explore your own relationship to loss as it relates to your trauma history.

- **Denial:** You can think of denial as a protective mechanism that buffers you from the reality of trauma. You might feel as though life is surreal. At times, you might feel disoriented or have an inability to concentrate. In the context of C-PTSD, denial can be expressed as dissociation; it's a way to live as if the event didn't happen or as if you weren't impacted.
- **Anger:** It is common to experience anger, rage, resentment, and blame. You might feel abandoned, powerless, and helpless. Grief brings up unfulfilled hopes and wishes that things had been different. You might miss someone who'd been there for you, but now is gone. Or you might miss the chance to connect with some someone who hadn't been there for you. It is common to have regret and lingering resentment. You might feel angry at yourself, your loved ones, or life itself.
- **Bargaining:** The core emotion of bargaining is guilt. You might relate to self-blaming statements such as "I should have been able to stop them from fighting," or "If only I had done something I could have prevented the abuse." Bargaining is characterized by magical thinking and beliefs that you can some-how turn back time to make a different, often unrealistic choice.
- **Depression:** Grief is most recognizable in deep sadness. However, with depression there is an accompanying despair or feeling, as though your life is meaningless. You might ask yourself, "What is the point of living?" You might wonder how you can go on or why you should. Recognize that this is not some-thing to fix directly; rather, it is the warning sign of what needs attending to—the feeling of emptiness that accompanies great loss.
- **Acceptance:** Acceptance is the ability to acknowledge what happened to you and to choose to live your life. This does not mean that you will feel okay about what happened. However, you can still invest in and find joy in your current relationships and engage in the world in a meaningful way.
- **Resilience and growth:** Anger, fear, and sadness are not the only emotions asso-ciated with a traumatic history—it is also possible to feel profound appreciation for your life. As a result of your unique life experiences, you might experience a deeper capacity to connect to others in meaningful ways, have an increased willingness to be vulnerable, or be more willing to ask for help. Resilience is not innate; it is learned and developed as part of the healing process.

IN PRACTICE

The goal of this practice is to work with conflicting emotions of resentment, regret, appreciation, and hope that are associated with grieving traumatic losses. This exercise has four sentence prompts. As you look at each one, take as much time as you need to write down any memories, reflections, words, and feelings that come to your mind.

What I feel grief about is . . .

_____

_____

_____

I feel anger and resentment about . . .

_____

_____

_____

What I regret is . . .

_____

_____

_____

My hope is . . .

_____

_____

_____

What I appreciate and accept is . . .

_____

_____

_____

When There Are No Words

Kathy often had powerful emotions and sensations in her body. She had a chronic tightness in her stomach and had been diagnosed with irritable bowel syndrome. She had unrelenting lower back pain. She had lived with these pains for so long, she assumed that change was impossible.

We began to work with the feelings in her body. I encouraged Kathy to focus her attention on her belly and lower back with mindfulness and curiosity. At first she began to cry. I invited her to continue to notice any emotions, images, words, or impulses to move her body.

Kathy said, "It is dark. I can't move! I feel stuck and my body hurts." She collapsed into the couch.

I reminded Kathy that she was in the safety of my office. She opened her eyes and looked around. She looked at me. Then I asked her to check back in with her sensations. She said, "I can feel my feet pushing against the floor. I notice a lump in my throat."

I then inquired, "What does your body want to do now?"

Kathy asserted, "I want to push and kick! I want to scream, 'Get away from me!'"

With encouragement she repeated these words. She slowly and mindfully pushed with her arms and legs. She allowed herself to intently repeat the words, "Get away from me!"

After several minutes Kathy became quiet. She looked peaceful and had a glow on her face that I hadn't seen before. She looked up at me and said, "It's over now."

She then remarked, "All of these years I had been telling the story from my head but I never let my body tell the story. I didn't know that my body had a story too!"

In the last decade, somatic psychotherapy has come to the forefront of therapies that treat PTSD. Dr. van der Kolk's book, *The Body Keeps the Score*, describes the science behind why the body needs to be included in treatment. For instance, early childhood memories prior to the age of five are not like typical memories that occur later in life. You tend not to have images or a clear story. Traumatic memories from after the age of five can also be repressed or dissociated from and recalled only in fragments. In either case, you might experience emotions without understanding why, or physical sensations of unknown origin. Therefore, reason and logic alone are seldom sufficient to treat trauma. Unresolved trauma impacts health, leading to a wide range of illnesses, including digestive problems, heart disease, cancer, chronic lung disease, liver disease, and autoimmune conditions, to name a few. Attending to the sensations and movement impulses of your body is a central part of healing.

> "Every bad feeling is potential energy toward a more right way of being if you give it space to move toward its rightness."
> —DR. EUGENE GENDLIN, philosopher and psychotherapist

THE BODY'S STORY

One limitation of talk therapy is the focus on telling the story in the past tense. Somatic psychotherapies engage body awareness in the here and now. All stressful life events evoke a fight-or-flight response. In situations of a threat without an escape, the body will freeze into immobilization.

You can unwind the physiological impact of traumatic events by sensing, breathing into, and moving your body. Somatic Experiencing therapy calls this process completing "unfinished defensive actions," in which you mindfully sense your need to have run away or fought back for survival. Sensorimotor psychotherapy sees the clenching of the jaw, tightened fists, or pursing of the lips as signals of incomplete actions that can be mindfully explored. As you allow your body to tell the story, you reclaim your capacity for healing movement. Ask yourself, "What wants to happen in my body now?" Then, mindfully draw your awareness to your sensations.

IN PRACTICE

Typically, depression as it relates to C-PTSD is connected to a lingering feeling of collapse in the body in response to feeling immobilized, helpless, or ashamed. The following Somatic Experiencing practice allows you to mindfully reclaim a sense of resiliency and strength in your body:

- Find a safe place to explore this practice. Sit in a chair.
- Allow yourself to collapse. Your shoulders might go forward and your gaze downward. Rather than fight against the collapse, allow yourself to mindfully exaggerate the collapse a little bit at a time until you are slumped forward over your legs.
- Take your time, and notice how you feel in your body. What emotions or thoughts arise?
- Then, just as slowly, lengthen your spine back up. Slowly lift your torso and your head until you are sitting tall with your head balanced at the top of your spine. Lift your gaze to look straight ahead of you. Feel the sensations in your chest. Do you notice any openness or expansion? What are the emotions or thoughts that arise now?
- If you feel the impulse to collapse again, then repeat these steps several more times until you feel that staying upright does not require so much effort.

Take a few moments to write about your experience with this body-centered practice.

_____

_____

_____

_____

_____

_____

_____

_____

_____

Mind and Body in Healing

One day, Kathy came into my office more uplifted. She shared that she attended several yoga classes in the past week. During her first class, she could only perform a small portion of the demanding physical practice. However, she described a remarkable experience—she felt "more confident."

Kathy said, "I stood a little taller and I felt more like myself the rest of the day."

Kathy also shared that she felt hopeful, and returned to yoga a few days later. Again, she felt both focused and relaxed afterward.

In the months following that session, Kathy began to practice yoga regularly. She shared that the positive effect seemed to increase when she challenged herself in standing postures for at least a portion of each class. She was slowly reclaiming her physical strength, flexibility, and capacity for rest.

As revealed by the ACE study (page 37), unresolved childhood trauma takes a significant toll on physical health. Stress and trauma-related diseases are associated with chronic dysregulation of the ANS; these include high blood pressure, blood sugar imbalances, immune system problems, and digestion disturbances. Therapeutic insight is an important part of the healing journey, but is generally insufficient to address the physical health implications of C-PTSD.

Many clients with a trauma history have difficulties with physical and emotional pain, and as a result, turn to rely upon medical doctors for help. Doctors and psychiatrists often prescribe medications, sometimes as a standalone treatment, and sometimes in addition to a referral for psychotherapy. For many years, medications such as benzodiazepines (Valium, Xanax, Ativan, Klonopin) have been prescribed because of their fast-acting properties on both physical and emotional pain. However, since 2012, this class of medications has been reclassified as contraindicated for PTSD because they are highly addictive and prolong the healing process. These medications can suppress the very physiological and psychological processes necessary to facilitate trauma resolution.

> "All of these years I had been telling the story from my head but I never let my body tell the story. I didn't know that my body had a story too!"

Medications for PTSD with promising results and fewer side effects are the class of SSRI medications (Prozac, Celexa, Zoloft, Paxil). In addition, a wide range of complementary and alternative medicine (CAM) interventions also prove to be tremendously beneficial for trauma recovery. Many clients find massage, acupuncture, meditation, yoga, exercise, and healthy nutrition to be integral to their well-being. Integrating regular exercise and restful relaxation into your daily routine can be essential for mind-body health.

VAGUS NERVE STIMULATION

Mind-body therapies work by regulating your ANS. The vagus nerve plays a central role. Healthy *vagal tone* keeps your digestive system functioning optimally, facilitates heart health, and keeps your immune system in check. Your vagus nerve passes through your belly, diaphragm, lungs, throat, inner ear, and facial muscles. Therefore, actions that influence these areas of your body can influence the functioning of the vagus nerve through the mind-body feedback loop. You can think of the vagus nerve as a two-way radio communication system helping you stay in touch with your sensations and emotions. Practices that stimulate the vagus nerve are aimed toward either relaxing or re-energizing yourself, depending upon what is needed to feel calm and in control. Vagus nerve stimulation can be achieved through strategies you can explore from the comfort of your home, including:

- **Humming:** The vagus nerve passes by the vocal cords and the inner ear. The vibrations of humming can soothe your nervous system. Pick your favorite tune and notice the sensations in your chest, throat, and head.
- **Conscious breathing:** Slow, conscious breathing is one of the fastest ways to influence our nervous system states. The aim is to move the belly and diaphragm with your breath and slow down your breathing. Vagus nerve stimulation occurs when the breath is slowed down from the typical 10 to 14 breaths per minute to 5 to 7 breaths per minute.
- **Valsalva maneuver:** This complicated name refers to a simple process of attempting to exhale against a closed airway. You can do this by keeping your mouth closed and pinching your nose while trying to breathe out. This increases the pressure inside the chest cavity, increasing vagal tone.
- **Diving reflex:** Considered a first-rate vagus nerve stimulation technique, splashing cold water on your face from your lips to your scalp line stimulates the diving reflex. You can also achieve the cooling effect by placing ice cubes in a zip-top bag and holding the ice against your face while briefly holding your breath. The diving reflex slows the heart rate, increases blood flow to the brain, reduces anger, and relaxes the body.

IN PRACTICE

What forms of exercise do you enjoy? What helps you relax? What additional supports do you think you need to achieve optimal health? (Massage, acupuncture, nutritional counseling, exercise trainer)

_____

_____

_____

_____

_____

_____

Look over the practices to stimulate your vagus nerve. Experiment with these practices. Become mindful and curious about your experience. For example, how long do you need to practice deep breathing until you feel a shift internally? Do you prefer humming or deep breathing? What did you discover?

_____

_____

_____

_____

_____

Anchoring Insights into Action

Kathy's symptoms of depression continued to improve. She no longer carried a core belief of herself as damaged, nor was she plagued by feelings of hopelessness. Sometimes she struggled with allowing herself to experience positive emotions like joy and happiness, but she learned to remind herself that she deserves to feel good.

Kathy recognized that her physical symptoms of stomach and back pain might not go away completely, but she felt less fearful of her pain. When she felt pain, she took it as a signal to slow down, breathe deeply, and check in with her body. She continued to practice yoga regularly and learned to carefully attend to her diet.

Now Kathy could say, "I am strong and capable. While I wish I had not had so much pain in my life, I no longer feel that my past will keep me from living a good and meaningful future."

Kathy felt open to the possibility of taking new risks. She could imagine investing in her friendships and that she might begin dating again. She took a deep breath and considered the possibilities ahead.

New positive beliefs and emotions are a common outcome of processing trauma. It is important to take the time to integrate positive emotions into your life. You deserve and are worthy of love and care. The integration phase of trauma treatment involves strengthening positive feelings and behaviors so you can feel capable of creating the life you want. Allowing positive feelings to grow requires tolerating the sensations that accompany emotions—even good ones such as joy, happiness, and excitement. Just like a ship is anchored close to shore to ensure easy access, you can create anchors for positive feelings and actions. Anchors can be simple statements or actions you take throughout your day that help you feel grounded and hopeful. For example, each morning when you wake up you could say to yourself, "I am enough." You could write this on a sticky note and place this on your mirror to see each morning. Or an anchor might be taking five deep breaths before each meal, reminding yourself to slow down and savor your meal.

Integration can also help you to gather courage and believe in yourself when you face a challenge. For instance, imagine that you want to ask your boss for a raise. You can visualize yourself standing tall, looking your boss in the eyes, and speaking confidently. You can imagine how you might feel if your boss says yes, and how you might handle the situation if your boss says no. In general, the process of integration focuses on strengthening your positive beliefs as they relate to your past, present, and future.

TOLERATING POSITIVE EMOTIONS

If you have experienced childhood neglect or abuse, it is unlikely that you had caregivers who supported your feelings of joy, happiness, or excitement. Worse, you may have even been punished for expressing your enthusiasm or exuberance. As a result, it can be difficult to tolerate these positive emotions in adulthood. You may have difficulty remembering good times or want to shut down when you feel pleasurable sensations.

You wouldn't criticize a flower in full bloom for taking up too much space, or a sunset for being too bright. But how many times have you dulled your own brilliance for fear that people might criticize you for being selfish or conceited? Or maybe you hold a belief that celebrating a good thing might make it go away. Perhaps guilt interferes with your ability to feel joy. Being selfish tends to be considered bad; however, psychologists have identified that a healthy form of selfishness is a key to well-being. Healthy selfishness is akin to self-care and doesn't mean that you do not care for other people. Rather, this form of selfishness is especially important for healing C-PTSD—it asks you to respect your needs and feelings even when others do not. Research shows that:

> Healthy selfishness is akin to self-care and doesn't mean that you do not care for other people. Rather, this form of selfishness is especially important for healing C-PTSD—it asks you to respect your needs and feelings even when others do not.

- **Selfish people are healthier.** They tend to take better care of themselves.
- **Selfish people have better relationships.** They have a well-developed sense of self, the ability to communicate, and uphold clear boundaries.
- **Selfish people make natural leaders.** They have a drive to succeed, confidence, and motivation to reach for their goals.
- **Selfish people are happier.** They spend their time doing pleasurable activities and are more authentic as a result.

It is time to reclaim your own capacity to bloom fully. You have the right to linger and luxuriate in the beauty of who you are. Pleasurable emotions are also shown to support a healthy immune system. So go ahead, say yes to that which truly nourishes you, express your creativity, and reflect on that which inspires you. What evokes a feeling of awe? Is it the sound of children laughing, the way light falls upon flowers in a garden, or the savory taste of chocolate on your tongue? Invite yourself to slow down and receive the gifts of the moment.

IN PRACTICE

This mindfulness practice offers an invitation to increase your awareness of positive sensations in your body. It can sometimes take practice to override the tendency to focus on discomfort or pain. If you find yourself distracted by painful sensations, be gentle and compassionate with yourself and the practice—it will get easier over time.

- **Notice ease:** Scan your body for a specific area where you feel good, at ease, and relaxed. If you have difficulty finding an area that is pain-free, take your attention further to your periphery and seek to identify an area of your body that feels neutral, such as the tip of your nose or your fingers and toes.
- **Expand and enjoy:** Breathe deeply into the sensations of ease or neutrality. What are the qualities of your sensations? Is there a temperature, a color, or an image that accompanies them? Can you allow the sensations of ease and relaxation to grow stronger? Perhaps you notice feelings of warmth or joy. Imagine these feelings spreading and filling your entire body. Stay with the process for as long as you like. Tell yourself there is no rush. Relax into joy.
- **Refocus and refine:** If you get distracted or feel "stuck in your head," gently bring your attention back to the specific area of ease that you started with. Repeat the process. Invite yourself to stay with positive sensations longer each time.

Take a few moments to write about your experience with this practice focusing on positive sensations and ease.

_____

_____

_____

_____

INSTALLING POSITIVE BELIEFS

EMDR therapy has an "installation phase" of treatment. This phase focuses on the integration of new positive beliefs about yourself into the past, present, and future. The first step asks you to imagine what it would feel like to know, without a doubt, that you are strong, worthy, capable, or powerful as you reflect on the traumatic memories of your childhood. You then take the time to let the positive belief about yourself grow in that context and to work through any barriers that interfere with your beliefs about yourself.

For example, perhaps you once believed that you were at fault for the events of your childhood. In this process, you can imagine seeing yourself as a child in those painful situations and tell that young part of you, "It was never your fault. You didn't do anything wrong. You are lovable just as you are." The second step involves imagining what your life today would be like if you fully believed in your own worthiness—if you trusted that you could be loved fully for who you are. The third step involves imagining how these positive beliefs about yourself can shape your future.

IN PRACTICE

Take a look at this list of positive beliefs:

- I am lovable
- I am important
- I am worthy
- I survived

- I am strong
- I am capable
- I belong
- I am safe now

Choose from this list or identify any other positive statements that feel most relevant to your healing process. Imagine that you could travel back in time and have a conversation with a younger version of yourself. Tell this younger self what you now know. You might say something like, "I know you think that it will always feel this bad, but I want you to know that you will survive this. There will be a time when you are safe. Even if you don't know it now, you are very important and worthy of love." Take your time to anchor your positive beliefs about yourself into the past.

"Our deepest fear is not that we are inadequate. Our deepest fear is that we are powerful beyond measure. It is our light, not our darkness that most frightens us. We ask ourselves, who am I to be brilliant, gorgeous, talented, fabulous? Actually, who are you *not* to be?"

—MARIANNE WILLIAMSON,
author and lecturer

Now, imagine bringing your words into your life right now. See yourself in your home or at work. You can say something like, "Sometimes life still feels hard but I know that the worst is over. I am safe now. I am important and worthy of love."

Finally, imagine yourself in the future. What goals do you have for yourself? Perhaps you can even visualize yourself successfully overcoming a challenge. You might imagine saying to your future self, "You are important and worthy of love. You are strong and capable. I believe in you and am so proud of your achievements."

Take a few moments to write about your experience with this practice.

_____

_____

_____

_____

Chapter Takeaways

This chapter guided you to work through the depressive symptoms of complex PTSD. You explored the issues of shame, helplessness, and dissociation. You attended to your grief. You learned ways to regulate your nervous system and to support your physical health. Moreover, you learned how to strengthen and anchor new positive feelings and beliefs about yourself into your life. Take the next several minutes to review the In Practice sections throughout this chapter and any notes you have written. What have you learned about yourself? Use this writing space as an opportunity to reflect on your experience thus far.

6

CHAPTER SIX

Supporting Long-Term Growth

Throughout this workbook, you have been asked to change your relationship to pain. Rather than resisting difficult emotions or memories, you faced your challenges. Hopefully, you feel stronger and you have deepened your self-understanding through engagement with the practices. The healing does not end here—it will continue beyond your time spent with this book. Emotional and physical well-being are best served when you actively participate in health-promoting behaviors each and every day. Ralph Waldo Emerson originated the now-famous saying, "Life is a journey, not a destination." I invite you to think about the healing journey as a deeply rewarding, lifelong process of self-discovery.

Within this final chapter, you will have opportunities to learn exercises that support personal growth and resilience. You will explore your relationship to your own creativity. You will foster compassion through forgiveness and gratitude. By developing a personal practice ritual, you will anchor your accomplishments into sustained change, or as B. K. S. Iyengar says, transformation.

Resilience and Growth

Research has studied the beliefs and behaviors of individuals who have not only survived but thrived in the aftermath of a traumatic childhood. The term *resilient* means adapting well in the face of adversity. This doesn't mean you don't experience distress; rather, resilience develops as a result of having sufficient support to work through difficult emotions. As a result, you cultivate a deepened self-understanding. Remember, resilience is not a trait that you either have or don't have; it's the result of learned strategies and practices.

> "Change leads to disappointment if it is not sustained. Transformation is sustained change, and it is achieved through practice."
> —B. K. S. IYENGAR, yoga master

You have practiced strategies to cultivate self-acceptance, develop mindfulness, increase emotion regulation, and cultivate healthy interpersonal relationships. All of these skills support resilience and growth. Resilience expert Dr. Jane McGonigal suggests that you grow stronger by identifying activities that support you physically, emotionally, mentally, socially, and spiritually. While each one of your action steps might seem small, collectively they can help you to feel strong, courageous, and capable.

Let's take a closer look at three of the primary aspects of resilience:

- **Connection:** Resilience is associated with having support from another person who can help you process difficult life events. This often comes in the form of psychotherapy; however, resilient people also actively build their social circle and stay involved with their community rather than isolating themselves.

- **Choice and control:** Childhood trauma can strip you of your sense of choice and control. You did not get a say in what happened to you then. Resilience is associated with an understanding that, with effort, you can influence the course of your life now. Focus on the events in your life that you do have control over presently.
- **Growth orientation:** Resilient people often believe that growth and wisdom can be gained from both positive and negative life experiences. They recognize that life offers ongoing opportunities for new learning.

Having any sort of trauma history provides you with an important perspective about life. Your difficult experiences can give you an increased willingness to reach out to others and ask for or accept help in vulnerable ways. Many with a trauma history share a deep empathy for humanity and develop a desire to help others or stand up against social injustices. In time, resilience is about becoming less defined by your history so you can bring your unique gifts and strengths into this world.

> Attend to your roots, but remember that you have a choice about what seeds to plant now.

IN PRACTICE

Explore your own relationship to resilience.

In what ways can you actively build your social connections? Do you make phone calls and reach out? Do you attend community events? In what ways can you strengthen your connections with others?

_____

_____

_____

_____

In what areas of your life do you feel like you have choices now? If you were to exercise, would you prefer to take a walk, go to the gym, or attend a yoga class? When you have free time, would you rather call a friend, read a favorite book, or write in your journal? What are the choices that best support your life right now?

_____

_____

_____

_____

_____

_____

_____

_____

In what ways have you grown as a result of your traumatic history? How have your difficult life events strengthened you? In what ways have your unique life experiences informed your understanding of yourself and the world?

_____

_____

_____

_____

_____

Courage to Create

Creativity, whether in the form of painting, dance, music, or other outlets, offers another way to process vulnerable emotions and, as a result, builds resilience. Any form of art can offer a portal to places beyond conceptual ideas. Painting can help you give color and shape to memories that are too difficult to put into words. Listening to a beautiful piece of music can inspire and awaken tender places in the heart. Poetry gives an expressive voice through language not comprised of everyday words. Poet Joy Harjo writes, "It was the spirit of poetry who reached out and found me as I stood there at the doorway between panic and love."

Art can also be a refuge—a relief from the intense emotions associated with healing trauma. For instance, a creative act can connect you to positive life experiences and reduce preoccupation with your trauma history. You might encounter a rush of joy, or a sense of identity that's not defined by your difficult past. Creative expression has been shown to reduce stress, improve self-esteem, and strengthen physical health outcomes.

Lastly, art provides opportunities to connect with others. Like an audience giving a standing ovation after a powerful performance, the experience of connecting to others through art is powerfully moving. Art joins us, body, mind, and soul. For instance, in a choir, each singer's heart rate actually slows down and synchronizes into a shared rhythm with the others. Many cultures come together in community rituals of drumming, singing, and dancing as a way to process grief and loss. Processing trauma through art within a group setting can provide a reminder that you are not alone— that everyone feels loss and pain. Importantly, for the most authen-

> "One can choose to go back toward safety or forward toward growth. Growth must be chosen again and again; fear must be overcome again and again."
> —DR. ABRAHAM MASLOW, psychologist

tic and therefore therapeutic experience, give yourself permission to create art based on what feels right to you, rather than worrying about what someone else will think. It is the process, not the product, that is important.

IN PRACTICE

Mindfully explore your relationship to art. In what ways do you express your creativity? What art forms inspire you? If you were to get in touch with your creativity now, what would you do? Need some ideas? You could write or read a poem. Choose a piece of music that opens your heart. Put on some music and dance in your living room. When was the last time you gave yourself permission to be creative?

_____

_____

_____

_____

_____

Suffering and Compassion

There is a story about a woman who visited the Buddha while deep in sadness and despair. She asked why she had to face such hardship and loss. In response, the Buddha asked her to go and get a grain of rice from each house in the village in which no loss had occurred or tears had been shed. She went from house to house, and after a week returned with an empty bowl. In realizing that she was not alone, she was transformed. Her suffering, which once caused her to feel isolated and hopeless, now became a gateway to compassion and connection.

Just as this woman came to understand she was not alone in her sadness, your suffering can serve as the foundation of personal transformation. According to neuropsychologist and meditation teacher Dr. Rick Hanson, compassion is genuine concern for the suffering of all beings, including yourself. Empathy allows you to imagine or feel the experience of another person and provides the groundwork for compassion. Two strategies that can build compassion are forgiveness and gratitude.

FORGIVENESS

Compassion is developed through practicing forgiveness. Resentments can weigh heavy not only on the mind, but also on physical health. Chronic anger keeps you in fight or flight and increases your risk for heart disease and diabetes. Research from The John Hopkins Hospital found that forgiveness practices lower the risk of heart attack, improve cholesterol levels, improve sleep, reduce pain, and decrease reported symptoms of anxiety and depression. Forgiveness is an act of letting go of your own negative feelings, whether or not the other person deserves it.

> "The creative act rises out of the struggle of human beings."
>
> —DR. ROLLO MAY, psychologist and author

Forgiveness is not a forced process. It is a choice. Forgiveness asks you to reflect deeply on harmful actions, yours and those of others. You start by forgiving yourself for the ways that you have caused harm. As you reflect on others' harmful actions, you might find that people hurt others because they were once hurt, were afraid, or were in pain. You also begin to recognize that another person's harmful actions are not a reflection of your own worth. You arrive at an understanding that no one is perfect.

IN PRACTICE

Write a letter about a situation you are struggling with. This letter can be to yourself or to another person. Take a moment to reflect on the situation and the hurt. What thoughts come to mind? What emotions are you aware of? Ask yourself if you are ready to forgive. If the answer is yes, express your forgiveness and the reasons behind your decision. If you are struggling with this practice, what support do you need to help heal your pain? If the letter is written to another person, you can either choose to mail the letter or place the letter in a drawer. Either way, this practice is for you and your therapeutic use as you learn to process forgiveness.

GRATITUDE

You cannot exempt yourself from difficult life experiences or painful emotions, but you can take a pause to focus on gratitude. It is difficult to feel thankful and stressed at the same time. Fight or flight can interfere with the quiet, reflective space required to feel grateful. However, focusing your mind on gratitude can help get you out of your stress response and build positive emotions such as joy, optimism, and happiness. Research suggests that having a regular gratitude practice strengthens the immune system and lowers blood pressure. The goal of any gratitude practice is to generate uplifting emotions, but not to force them if you are not feeling them authentically.

Research out of the Greater Good Science Center at University of California, Berkeley, suggests maintaining a daily "three good things" practice, in which you keep a journal devoted to positive aspects of your life. Every evening, you write down three things that went well, with details about how each made you feel. A second recommended practice is to take a "savoring walk," in which you walk outside, observing the sights, sounds, and smells. Each time you have a positive experience, take the time to really feel and absorb the sensations and emotions.

> Forgiveness is an act of letting go of your own negative feelings, whether or not the other person deserves it.

IN PRACTICE

Try this three-part gratitude practice:

Find a quiet place where you can sit and reflect. If you like, bring your hands over your heart and take a deep breath. Allow your mind to settle down and appreciate the experience of coming to rest. Bring to mind an intention to spend the next several minutes focused on gratitude for the people, experiences, and things in your life.

- **Part I** is for you. Start by taking a few breaths to appreciate you. Thank yourself for making time and space for this practice. Extend this positive feeling even further by appreciating one aspect of you: maybe your legs for carrying you through the world, your smile, or an act of compassion you offered to another.
- **Part II** is for someone else in your life. Turn your mind to a person or people who have been kind to you, and take a deep breath into your heart. Maybe you think about a relative who helped care for you, a neighbor who is always willing to lend a helping hand, or even a stranger who performed a random act of kindness. Take a deep breath as you give thanks for someone who made a difference in your life.
- **Part III** is for your surroundings. Turn your mind to one thing you appreciate in the world around you. Perhaps you focus on feeling grateful for the home in which you live. Maybe you focus your attention on something in the natural world that you are thankful for, such as the beauty of a sunset, or trees that bring us shade, or the earth that holds us all.

Take as long as you like, repeating all three steps as often as suits you. When you are finished, take a final few moments to consider how you feel before stepping back out into the world. Perhaps you notice feelings of warmth or positivity; however, if you are not feeling grateful, it's important to know that you are not failing at this practice. Make space for whatever you feel. Attending to your authentic experience is the most important part of the practice.

Developing a Personal Practice

Research suggests that repeated practice is necessary in order to establish healthy habits. Developing a new routine requires at least several months, if not a year, of regular commitment to your desired goals. I encourage you to continue the mindfulness practices and resources found within this workbook in the coming months. It can be beneficial to develop a personal practice routine for your self-care. For example, you might find it helpful to set aside a regular time each day to journal, practice yoga, or exercise. Also, gauge whether you prefer to practice alone at home or with others in a public class. If you find it difficult to create time for your self-care, you can start small with 5 or 10 minutes each day—every bit helps. Once you find a routine you enjoy, it is natural to want to extend your practice time longer.

IN PRACTICE

Think about what kind of personal self-care practices you would like to bring into your life. What time of day is the best time for you to practice? Do you want to be alone or with others? What support do you need for your self-care practice?

_____

_____

_____

_____

_____

_____

_____

_____

RESOURCES IN REVIEW

When you are feeling depressed or anxious, it can be hard to remember the positive actions you can take to soothe yourself. Yet, it is when you are at these low points that you need your resources the most. This list contains all the resources that you have explored within this workbook—in one place. Add on to this list and personalize it by adding any other positive thoughts, images, or actions. For example, perhaps you enjoy going on hikes, spending time by the ocean, watching movies, or taking baths. Make copies so you'll have this list accessible whenever needed. You can place copies in your wallet or purse, or on your refrigerator.

My Resources

- Replace negative self-statements with positive beliefs.
- Challenge thinking errors with disputing questions (Do I know for certain that the worst will happen?)
- Visualize a safe or peaceful place.
- Mindfully scan your body, attending to sensations with curiosity and self-acceptance.
- Consciously breathe with a 4-count inhale and 4-count exhale.
- Half-smile to cultivate a sense of serenity.
- Replace an outgrown habit with a positive behavior.
- Seek, identify, and visit a healing space in your home.
- Identify when you are emotionally hijacked and slow yourself down with 5 slow, deep breaths.
- Ground yourself by feeling your feet on the earth and releasing your weight into gravity.
- Name five things you see, four things you hear, three things you can touch, two things you can smell, and take one deep slow breath.
- Practice vagus nerve stimulation (e.g., humming, Valsalva maneuver, diving reflex).
- Place distressing feelings into your imagined container.
- Imagine nurturing or protective allies.
- Give yourself positive messages about your emotions (e.g., "I can allow my feelings to come and go like waves in the ocean").
- Replace "I am sad" with "I feel sad."
- Avoid saying "should" to yourself.
- Talk back to shame or your inner critic as if you were standing up to a bully.
- Reassert healthy boundaries by saying no or asking for what you need.
- Engage in healthy communication for conflict resolution (e.g., stay descriptive, name your feelings, ask for what you want, listen to what they need, be gentle, etc.).
- Allow yourself to be vulnerable.

- Reach out for connection by making a phone call or getting together with a friend.
- Pendulate your awareness between distressing and calming sensations.
- Allow space for grief.
- Journal about difficult life events.
- Write a forgiveness letter to yourself or another person.
- Journal about gratitude (three good things).
- Go for a savoring walk.
- Focus on positive sensations in your body and allow them to grow.
- Engage in a creative activity (paint, make music, dance, write a poem).
- Practice mindfulness through meditation, yoga, qigong, or tai chi.

_____

_____

_____

_____

_____

_____

_____

_____

_____

_____

_____

_____

_____

_____

_____

Final Reflections

Think of wisdom, compassion, hope, and joy as flowers that come from a well-tended garden. Attend to your roots, but remember that you have a choice about what seeds to plant now. To care for your precious piece of earth you must, at times, pull up the weeds. Shed the remnants of unworthiness, helplessness, and shame. Place them in the compost, where, in that darkness your grief can transform them into nutrient-rich soil. Plant loving thoughts and sow seeds of positivity. Allow the seeds of kindness to grow. Nurture them with self-care. As you nourish yourself, you'll cultivate peace. You'll grow yourself beautiful. To bloom is to open your heart to the world, fully and unapologetically. Are you willing to open up to this world, knowing that pain and heartache will happen? Maybe not today, and that's okay. It's a journey. Continue to pursue your beautiful self. Continue to be kind to yourself. Return to this book whenever you feel you need to circle back to the foundation of your self-understanding and healing. Like many things in this world, good things happen when we least expect it, and every step you take toward wholeness stacks those odds in your most deserving favor.

"The most beautiful people we have known are those who have known defeat, known suffering, known struggle, known loss, and have found their way out of the depths. These persons have an appreciation, a sensitivity, and an understanding of life that fills them with compassion, gentleness, and a deep loving concern. Beautiful people do not just happen."
—ELISABETH KÜBLER-ROSS, psychiatrist and author

Glossary

acceptance: Welcoming reality as it is without needing to resist or change it.

afflictive emotions: Feelings that create distortions in thinking and fatigue in the body.

agoraphobia: Extreme fear of crowded spaces or public places.

attachment: The emotional bond that occurs between two people, initially a caregiver and an infant, which provides a foundation for healthy relationships later in life.

autonomous nervous system: The part of the nervous system responsible for the parts of your body that you do not have conscious control over, such as your heart rate, breathing, and digestion.

avoidance: Learned patterns of shutting out or pushing away uncomfortable sensations, memories, or emotions; often maintained by defenses such as denial, repression, dissociation, or addictive behaviors.

coherence: Having a story about your life that helps you make sense of your life experiences.

containment: A resource for recovery involving the use of an imaginary container to hold unwanted or painful thoughts, feelings or memories.

continuum: A range of experiences that are related but slightly different from each other, often existing between two polarities or extremes.

depersonalization: Disconnecting from your feelings or thoughts as though they are not yours.

derealization: Feeling as though life is surreal or as if you are living in a dream.

desensitization: Reflecting on a traumatic event with sensory details, thoughts, and feelings resulting in a reduction of the amount of emotional and somatic distress associated with the traumatic event.

dialectic: A synthesis of opposites and a core aspect of Zen Buddhist practices.

dissociation: A biological protection that disconnects you from threatening experiences creating a division between the part of you involved in daily living and the part of you holding emotions of fear, shame, or anger.

dual awareness state: The act of remaining aware of present surroundings while simultaneously recalling memories of an earlier time.

ego states: Different parts of self that are developed to hold unwanted or unacceptable feelings and memories. In the context of C-PTSD, these are often parts that reflect younger developmental phases of life related to traumatic memories.

emotional dysregulation: Difficulty managing emotions, leading to reacting strongly or unpredictably to situations or people.

emotional hijacking: Strong emotions such as fear or anger initiate a fight-or-flight response that overpowers your upper brain centers and compromises your thoughts and behaviors.

emotional intelligence: The ability to identify and respond effectively to emotions—yours and those of the people around you.

emotion regulation: Responding effectively to strong feelings and urges. Regulation involves increasing conscious awareness about your thoughts, body sensations, and emotions so that you can be less reactive, ultimately giving you a greater ability to choose behaviors that best support you.

equanimity: The ability to stand in the middle of intensity, to develop patience with uncomfortable experiences, and to see the big picture as a way to maintain balance.

grounding: A resource for recovery that involves consciously sensing the body and feeling the feet on the earth to calm the nervous system.

high arousal symptoms: Sometimes referred to as hyperarousal; these symptoms are characterized by anxiety, hypervigilance, irritability, aggression, impulsiveness, and an exaggerated startle response.

hypervigilance: Being on guard or highly sensitized to your surroundings in order to keep yourself safe.

introject: Internalizing characteristics, attitudes, or ideas from other people into your own psyche. Often you turn the feelings you have about another toward yourself.

low arousal symptoms: Sometimes referred to as hypoarousal, these symptoms are characterized by depression, fatigue, lethargy, and feelings of despair, shame, or collapse.

pendulation: Alternating your attention between feelings of safety and feelings of distress as they are experienced in your body.

radical self-acceptance: Accepting reality as it is, rather than fighting it or lamenting its unfairness. This term is also used to describe unconditionally loving yourself inclusive of any faults and weaknesses.

relational trauma: Harm caused by one person to another that impairs a sense of safety in relationships.

self-efficacy: Your belief that you can, with effort, produce a desired outcome and influence the course of events in your life.

sequencing: A somatic psychology term that refers to the movement of tension out from the core of the body through the extremities of your arms and legs.

somatic: Relating to the body, especially as distinct from the mind.

vagus nerve: The cranial nerve that plays a central role in the regulation of the ANS because it connects your brain to your digestive system, heart, lungs, throat, and facial muscles.

window of tolerance: An optimal zone of nervous system arousal where you are able to respond effectively to your emotions.

Wise Mind: A cognitive behavioral therapy term that refers to an optimal balance of your thinking "reasonable mind," and your feeling "emotional mind"; an integration of logic and intuition.

Resources

The following books, online resources, and national hotlines are provided as resources for your continued healing of complex PTSD. Keep in mind that as you seek out healing resources, some of these will resonate for you and others may not. Choose the ones that feel supportive for you and that align with your own beliefs and values. Furthermore, online forums and blogs are not always well regulated. Because of the painful nature of complex PTSD, some sites might include content that is unfiltered and therefore triggering of your own history. Continue to pace yourself by choosing carefully what, when, and how much content to expose yourself to, so as not to feel re-traumatized during your healing process. Lastly, some websites will also offer unfounded opinions, misinformation, and bad advice from untrustworthy sources. Trust yourself—if it doesn't feel good to you, turn instead toward the resources that feel supportive of your process.

Books

Brach, Tara. *Radical Acceptance: Embracing Your Life with the Heart of a Buddha.* New York: Bantam, 2004.

Brown, Brené. *Daring Greatly: How the Courage to Be Vulnerable Transforms the Way We Live, Love, Parent, and Lead.* New York: Avery, 2015.

Brown, Brené. *The Gifts of Imperfection.* Center City, MN: Hazelden Publishing, 2010.

Covey, Stephen. *The 7 Habits of Highly Effective People: Powerful Lessons in Personal Change.* New York: Free Press, 2004.

Emerson, David, and Elizabeth Hopper. *Overcoming Trauma through Yoga: Reclaiming your Body*. Berkeley, CA: North Atlantic, 2012.

Goleman, Daniel. *Emotional Intelligence*. New York: Random House, 2006.

Hanson, Rick, and Richard Mendius. *Buddha's Brain: The Practical Neuroscience of Happiness, Love, & Wisdom*. Oakland, CA: New Harbinger, 2009.

Herman, Judith. *Trauma and Recovery: The Aftermath of Violence—from Domestic Abuse to Political Terror*. New York: Basic Books, 1992.

Kabat-Zinn, Jon. *Full Catastrophe Living*. New York: Bantam Books, 2009.

Kushner, Harold. *When Bad Things Happen to Good People*. Norwell, MA: Anchor Press, 2004.

Levine, P. *Healing Trauma: A Pioneering Program for Restoring the Wisdom of your Body*. Boulder, CO: Sounds True, 2008.

Maiberger, Barb. *EMDR Essentials: A Guide for Clients and Therapists*. New York: W. W. Norton & Co., 2009.

Mate, G. *When the Body Says No: Understanding the Stress-Disease Connection*. New York: Random House, 2011.

McGonigal, Jane. *Super Better: A Revolutionary Approach to Getting Stronger, Happier, Braver, and More Resilient*. New York: Penguin Press, 2015.

Miller, Alice. *The Drama of the Gifted Child: The Search for the True Self*. New York: Basic Books, 1997.

Pennebaker, James W., and John F. Evans. *Expressive Writing: Words that Heal*. Enumclaw, WA: Idyll Arbor, 2014.

Perry, Bruce, and Maia Szalavitz. *The Boy Who Was Raised as a Dog: And Other Stories from a Child Psychiatrist's Notebook*. New York: Basic Books, 2006.

Shapiro, Francine. *Getting Past Your Past: Take Control of Your Life with Self-Help Techniques from EMDR Therapy*. Emmaus, PA: Rodale, 2012.

Siegel, Daniel. *Mindsight: The New Science of Personal Transformation*. New York: Bantam, 2010.

van der Kolk, Bessel. *The Body Keeps the Score: Brain, Mind, and Body in the Healing of Trauma*. New York: Viking, 2014.

TED Talks:

Brené Brown: The power of vulnerability

Brené Brown: Listening to shame

Nadine Burke Harris: How childhood trauma affects health across a lifetime

Jane McGonigal: The game that can give you 10 extra years of your life

Kelly McGonigal: How to make stress your friend

Martin Seligman: The new era of positive psychology

Websites and Online Directories:

APA.org/topics/trauma: The American Psychological Association's resources for survivors and their loved ones

Goodtherapy.org: Therapist directory and blog

Griefshare.org: Directory of local grief support groups

Inspire.com: Online support groups and discussion community

NAMI.org: Website for National Alliance on Mental Illness (NAMI), with comprehensive information and additional online resources

Ok2talk.org: Online community for teens and young adults to share poetry and personal stories of recovery.

Psychcentral.com: Relevant articles and online community forums

Psychologytoday.com: Relevant articles and therapist directory

Self-injury.net: Information for recovery and online forum

Traumasurvivorsnetwork.org: Informational website with online support for survivors and their loved ones

National Hotlines

National Child Abuse Hotline: 800-422-4453 (800-4-A-CHILD)

National Domestic Violence Hotline: 800-799-7233 (800-799-SAFE)

National Parent Helpline: 855-427-2736 (855-4-A-PARENT)

National Suicide Prevention Lifeline: 800-273-8255 (800-273-TALK)

Trans Lifeline: 877-565-8860 (24/7 crisis support by and for the transgender community)

Trevor Lifeline: 866-488-7386 (24/7 crisis support for queer and questioning youth)

References

Allen, J. G. "Challenges in Treating Post-Traumatic Stress Disorder and Attachment Trauma." *Current Women's Health Reports* 3, no. 3 (June 2003): 213–20.

Brach, T. *Radical Acceptance: Embracing Your Life with the Heart of a Buddha*. New York: Bantam, 2004.

Burke, N. J., J. L. Hellman, B. G. Scott, C. F. Weems, and V. G. Carrion. "The Impact of Adverse Childhood Experiences On an Urban Pediatric Population." *Child Abuse and Neglect* 35, no. 6 (2001): 408–13.

Courtois, Christine, and Julian Ford. *Treating Complex Traumatic Stress Disorders (Adults): Scientific Foundations and Therapeutic Models*. New York: Guilford, 2013.

Cromer, L. D., J. M. Smyth. "Making Meaning of Trauma: Trauma Exposure Doesn't Tell the Whole Story." *Journal of Contemporary Psychotherapy* 40, no. 2 (2010): 65–72.

Damasio, A. R. *The Feeling of What Happens: Body and Emotion in the Making of Consciousness*. New York: Harcourt, 2000.

Emerson, D., and E. Hopper. *Overcoming Trauma through Yoga: Reclaiming Your Body*. Berkeley, CA: North Atlantic, 2012.

Felitti, V. J., R. F. Anda, Dale Nordenberg, David Williamson, Alison Spitz, Valerie Edwards, Mary Koss, et al. "Relationship of Childhood Abuse and Household Dysfunction to Many of the Leading Causes of Death in Adults." *American Journal of Preventive Medicine* 14 (1998): 245-58.

Fonagy, P., Gyorgy Gergely, Elliot Jurist, and Mary Target. *Affect Regulation, Mentalization, and the Development of the Self*, New York: Other Press, 2002.

Frankl, V. *Man's Search for Meaning*. New York: Washington Square Press, 1963.

Gendlin, E. *Focusing*. New York: Bantam Books, 1982.

Groves, D. A., and V. J. Brown. "Vagal Nerve Stimulation: A Review of Its Applications and Potential Mechanisms that Mediate Its Clinical Effects." *Neuroscience Behavioral Review* 29, no. 3 (2005): 493-500.

Halifax, J. *The Fruitful Darkness: Reconnecting with the Body of the Earth*. New York: HarperCollins, 1993.

Hanson, R., and R. Mendius. *Buddha's Brain: The Practical Neuroscience of Happiness, Love, & Wisdom*. Oakland, CA: New Harbinger, 2009.

Harjo, J. *Crazy Brave: A Memoir*. New York: W. W. Norton & Co., 2013.

Heller, Rachael F., and Richard F. Heller. *Healthy Selfishness: Getting the Life your Deserve Without the Guilt*. New York: Meredith Books, 2006.

Herman, J. *Trauma and Recovery: The Aftermath of Violence—from Domestic Abuse to Political Terror*. New York: Basic Books, 1992.

Kabat-Zinn, Jon. *Full Catastrophe Living*. New York: Bantam Books, 2009.

Kessler, R. C., A. Sonnega, E. Bromet, M. Hughes, and C. B. Nelson. "Posttraumatic Stress Disorder in the National Comorbidity Survey." *Archives of General Psychiatry* 52, no. 12 (1995): 1048-60.

Knipe, J. *EMDR Toolbox: Theory and Treatment of Complex PTSD and Dissociation*. New York: Springer, 2014.

Korn, D. L. "EMDR and the Treatment of Complex PTSD: A Review." *Journal of EMDR Practice and Research* 3, no. 4 (2009): 264-78.

Kushner, H. *When Bad Things Happen to Good People*. Norwell, MA: Anchor Press, 2004.

Lally, P., Cornelia H. M. van Jaarsveld, Henry W. W. Potts, and Jane Wardle. "How Are Habits Formed: Modelling Habit Formation In the Real World." *European Journal of Social Psychology* 40, no. 6 (2010): 998-1009.

LeDoux, J. *Emotional Brain*. New York: Simon & Schuster, 1998.

Levine, P. *Healing Trauma: A Pioneering Program for Restoring the Wisdom of Your Body*. Boulder, CO: Sounds True, 2008.

Levine, P. *In an Unspoken Voice: How the Body Releases Trauma and Restores Goodness*. Berkeley: North Atlantic, 2010.

Levine, P. *Waking the Tiger: Healing Trauma: The Innate Capacity to Transform Overwhelming Experiences*. Berkeley: North Atlantic Books, 1997.

Linehan, M. M. *Skills Training Manual for Treating Borderline Personality Disorder*. New York: Guilford Press, 1993.

Luthar, S. S. *Resilience and Vulnerability*. Cambridge, UK: Cambridge Press, 2003.

Maddi, S. R. *Hardiness: Turning Stressful Circumstances into Resilient Growth*. New York: Springer, 2012.

Maiberger, B. *EMDR Essentials: A Guide for Clients and Therapists*. New York: W. W. Norton & Co., 2009.

Mate, G. *When the Body Says No: Understanding the Stress-Disease Connection*. New York: Random House, 2011.

McGonigal, J. *SuperBetter: A Revolutionary Approach to Getting Stronger, Happier, Braver, and More Resilient*. New York: Penguin Press, 2015.

Miller, A. *The Drama of the Gifted Child: The Search for the True Self*. New York: Basic Books, 1997.

Mugerwa, S., and J. D. Holden. "Writing Therapy: A New Tool for General Practice?" *British Journal of General Practice* 62, no. 605 (2012): 661–63.

Nugent. N. R., Ananda B. Amstadter, and Karestan C. Koenen. "Genetics of Post-Traumatic Stress Disorder: Informing Clinical Conceptualizations and Promoting Future Research." *American Journal of Medical Genetics* 148C, no. 2 (2008): 127–32.

Ogden, P., Kekuni Minton, and Clare Pain. *Trauma and the Body: A Sensorimotor Approach to Psychotherapy*. New York: W. W. Norton & Co., 2006.

Oliver, M. *Red Bird: Poems*. Boston: Beacon Press, 2009.

Pennebaker J. W. "Writing About Emotional Experiences as a Therapeutic Process." *Psychological Science* 18, no. 3 (1997): 162–66.

Perry, B., and M. Szalavitz. *The Boy Who Was Raised as a Dog: And Other Stories from a Child Psychiatrist's Notebook*. New York: Basic Books, 2006.

Pert, C. *Molecules of Emotion: The Science Behind Mind-Body Medicine*. New York: Scribner, 1997.

Rogers, C. A Way of Being. New York: Mariner, 1995.

Rothschild, B. *The Body Remembers: The Psychophysiology of Trauma and Trauma Treatment*. New York: W. W. Norton & Co., 2000.

Scaer, R. *The Trauma Spectrum: Hidden Wounds and Human Resiliency*. New York: W. W. Norton & Co., 2005.

Seligman, M. E. *Helplessness: On Depression, Development, and Death*. San Francisco: W. H. Freeman, 1992.

Shapiro, F. *Getting Past Your Past: Take Control of Your Life with Self-Help Techniques from EMDR Therapy*. Emmaus, PA: Rodale, 2012.

Shapiro, F. *Eye Movement Desensitization and Reprocessing: Basic Principles, Protocols and Procedures*. 2nd ed. New York: The Guilford Press, 2001.

Siegel, D. J. *The Developing Mind: How Relationships and the Brain Interact to Shape Who We Are*. New York: Guilford Press, 1999.

Siegel, D. *Mindsight: The New Science of Personal Transformation*. New York: Bantam Books, 2010.

Stellar, J. E., N. John-Henderson, C. L. Anderson, A. M. Gordon, G. D. McNeil, and D. Keltner. "Positive Affect and Markers of Inflammation: Discrete Positive Emotions Predict Lower Levels of Inflammatory Cytokines. *Emotion*, 15, no. 2 (2015): 129-33.

Stuckey, H. L., and J. Nobel. "The Connection Between Art, Healing, and Public Health: A Review of Current Literature." *American Journal of Public Health*, 100, no. 2 (2010): 254-63.

Substance Abuse and Mental Health Services Administration. *Trauma-Informed Care in Behavioral Health Services*. Treatment Improvement Protocol (TIP) Series 57. HHS Publication No. (SMA) 13-4801. Rockville, MD: Substance Abuse and Mental Health Services, Administration, 2014.

Toussaint, L. L., Everett L. Worthington, and David R. Williams, eds. *Forgiveness and Health: Scientific Evidence and Theories Relating Forgiveness to Better Health*. New York: Springer, 2015.

Updegraff, J. A., Roxane Silver, and E. Alision Holman. "Searching For and Finding Meaning in Collective Trauma: Results from A National Longitudinal Study of the 9/11 Terrorist Attacks. *Journal of Personality and Social Psychology* 95, no. 3 (2008): 709-22.

van der Hart, O., Ellert R. S. Nijenhuis, and Kathy Steele. *The Haunted Self: Structural Dissociation and the Treatment of Chronic Traumatization*. New York: Norton, 2006.

van der Kolk, B. A., L. Stone, J. West, A. Rhodes, D. Emerson, M. Suvak, and J. Spinazzola. "Yoga as an Adjunctive Treatment for Posttraumatic Stress Disorder." *Journal of Clinical Psychiatry* 75, no. 6 (2014): e559-e565.

van der Kolk, B. *The Body Keeps the Score: Brain, Mind, and Body in the Healing of Trauma.* New York: Viking, 2014.

Williamson, M. *A Return To Love: Reflections on the Principles of A Course in Miracles.* New York: Harper One, 1996.

Yehuda, R. "Neuroendocrine Alterations in Post-Traumatic Stress Disorder." *Primary Psychiatry* 9 (2002): 30-34.

Index

Diane's story, 17–18. *See also* case studies
digestive disturbances and sluggishness, 36
disassociation, understanding, 30
discrimination, 20
disgust, recognizing, 101
disorganized attachment style, 25
disorientation, 26
dissociation
    explained, 74
    healing, 133–134
    writing about, 135
distress tolerance, 46, 111–112. *See also* tolerable stress response
diving reflex, 144
domestic violence, 20, 37, 173
drug addiction, 117
DSM-5 (Diagnostic and Statistical Manual of Mental Disorders), 21
Duke, Marshall, 120
DVC (dorsal vagal complex), 57–58
dysphoria, 21

E

ease, noticing, 148
eating disorders, 27
EEG monitoring, 63
ego states, 53
eight phase treatment model, 49
Einstein, Albert, 76
EMDR (eye movement desensitization and reprocessing) therapy, 49–51, 122, 149
Emerson, Ralph Waldo, 153
emotion regulation, 46, 107–112
emotional and mental symptoms, 28–33
emotional distress, 26

emotional flooding, interrupting, 109
emotional hijacking, 108
emotional neglect, 37
emotional reasoning, 99
emotional symptoms, identifying, 31
empathy, 158
equanimity
    finding amidst change, 83
    regaining, 109
excitement and joy, recognizing, 101
exile part, 53
expand and enjoy, 148
exposure therapy, 43

F

family history, considering, 120
fantasy, 73
father, childhood relationship, 116
fear
    experiencing, 15
    growing up with, 16
    recognizing, 101
"felt sense," 30
fight-or-flight response, 34, 108, 160
firefighter part, 53
"flowers and stones," 63
food cravings, 36
forgiveness, 159–160
Frankl, Viktor E., 134, 136
Fred's story, 19. *See also* case studies
friendships, recalling from childhood, 118

G

Gendlin, Eugene, 140
goals, committing to, 161
Goldilocks principle, 59
Goleman, Daniel, 108
good versus bad, 97–98

gratitude, practicing, 160–161
Greater Good Science Center at University of California, 160
grief
    stages of, 136–137
    support groups, 173
    and trauma, 135–138
    writing about, 138
grounding, 52, 87–88
group therapy, 48
growth
    orientation, 155
    and resistance, 154–156
    stage of grief, 137

H

half-smile, engaging, 79
Hanson, Rick, 158
Harjo, Joy, 157
Hayes, Stephen, 63
healing
    childhood traumas, 11–12
    dissociation, 133–134
    journey, 153
    mind and body in, 142–145
    relationship, 45
    requirement, 42
    roadmap, 67–68
    shame, 131–133
healing allies, 90–91
healing space, 86. *See also* safe place in EMDR therapy
health problems, 27. *See also* unhealthy urges
Helen's story, 29. *See also* case studies
helplessness, learning, 129–130
Herman, Judith, 67
high blood pressure, 36
history. *See* personal history
hope
    thinking about, 165
    writing about, 138
hotlines, 173
humming, 144

W

websites and online directories, 172
will and surrender, balancing, 113
Williamson, Marianne, 150

window of tolerance, 110. *See also* tolerable stress response
Winnicott, D. W., 75
wisdom, 165
"Wise Mind," 46

X

Xanax, 143

Y

Yehuda, Rachael, 119
yoga, 60, 113

Z

Zen Buddhist philosophy, 45
Zoloft, 143

Acknowledgments

This book would have been impossible to complete without the loving support and encouragement of many important people in my life. I am grateful to my husband and two children. Thank you for your hard work and patience with me as I wrote, edited, and rewrote, birthing this book into being. Thank you for allowing our dining room table to be temporarily taken over by my computer, stacks of books, and papers. Thank you to my husband, Bruce, for your careful listening and editing support. I couldn't have written this book without the undying support of my parents, Carolyn and Victor. Thank you for believing in me so that I could believe in myself, and for reflecting my strength so that I can stand in my power. I owe a debt of gratitude to all of my mentors who have imparted your wisdom and compassion. In particular, to Betty Cannon and Jim Knipe, I thank you for your supervision and guidance, and for seeing me so clearly. I would also like to thank my friends and colleagues for being continual sources of inspiration and for standing with me as I take new steps personally and professionally. Lastly, I am in deep appreciation for my clients. Thank you for sharing with me your vulnerable, hurt places. You inspire me with your courage to face your fears and confront your darkest spaces. Thank you for your commitment to being real, and for allowing me to show up authentically with you. You are my teachers; this book is written for you.

About the Author

ARIELLE SCHWARTZ, PhD, is a licensed clinical psychologist, EMDR therapy consultant, and certified yoga instructor with a private practice in Boulder, Colorado. She earned her masters in somatic psychology through Naropa University and her doctorate in clinical psychology at Fielding Graduate University. Her strength-based approach to psychotherapy is called Resilience Informed Therapy, which integrates a mind-body approach to healing. She is a core teacher with the Maiberger Institute, offering therapist trainings in EMDR therapy and somatic psychology. She specializes in PTSD, complex PTSD, grief and loss, resilience in child development, therapeutic yoga, and healing chronic pain and illness. She believes all people deserve to be empowered by knowledge and is dedicated to offering informational mental health and wellness updates through her heartfelt community presentations, social media presence, and blog.

About the
Foreword Author

JIM KNIPE, PhD, has been a licensed psychologist in private practice in Colorado since 1976 and has been using EMDR since 1992. He was designated a Master Clinician by EMDRIA in 2007 and has served as keynote speaker at numerous national and international conferences. He is the author of the best-selling book, *EMDR Toolbox: Theory and Treatment for Complex PTSD and Dissociation.* Dr. Knipe is renowned for his exceptionally informed and compassionate therapeutic understanding of healing C-PTSD.